Monopoly and Social Control

Monopoly and Social Control

HENRY A. WELLS

Introduction by Wendell Berge

Public Affairs Press, Washington, D. C.

INTRODUCTION

Much has been written in recent years about the problems of monopoly and free competition. The fact that many scholars have become interested in the matter is a good omen. The studies of the Temporary National Economic Committee produced a wealth of factual material which brought into focus the questions that still remain to be solved — the questions of how to preserve a private competitive economy in the midst of a world that trends increasingly toward economic dictatorship.

We have found in this country that under the duress of war, depression or inflation, governmental controls over our economy are necessary. However, we have somehow always been able to terminate the controls when the crisis is past.

Henry A. Wells has written the most penetrating analysis of the economics of competition which I have read. His work is based on a deep understanding of the historical processes out of which political democracy and economic freedom have evolved. I have read most of the literature written in the last twenty years on the general subject of monopoly and competition. I can honestly say that Mr. Wells' book, *Monopoly and Social Control*, is the most illuminating document written in our time.

Mr. Wells for many years has been a tireless worker for the advancement of a philosophy which embodies the belief that the welfare of America, and, indeed, the world, lies in promoting political and economic institutions which allow the freest play of individual initiative. But this does not mean *laissez faire* in the traditional sense. Indeed, Mr. Wells recognizes the necessary role of government in protecting competition. The nub of the matter is this: competition without the protection of government tends in time to become monopolistic in itself. Therefore, government must be constantly present to prevent monopolistic aggregations from dominating the market. It should lay down rules which prevent monopoly, leaving the vast area of business activity free to employ its dynamic energies, subject only to the limitation that those energies shall not be used to suppress competition. This is the antithesis of regulation. And it is the philosophy which underlies the anti-trust laws, and, as I understand, is the basic credo of our country.

v

The course advocated in recent years by some of the so-called "planners", even though well-motivated, carries sinister implications. If we are to plan for a noble state, others having temporary political power might plan for an ignoble one. The equally infamous doctrines of Hitler and Stalin have been based on the notion that a government possessing total power will act for the best welfare of the people. These dogmas we reject.

My only concern is that the "defenders" of free enterprise have taken the defensive. We should not think in terms of "defending" the system; rather we should recognize that political democracy and free competitive enterprise represent the only dynamic forces left in the world. Mr. Wells' analysis demonstrates that the main hope for freedom rests on the promotion of policies which will keep the channels of competition free, and vigorously suppress monopolistic practices.

This book is rich in historical perspective, but it also displays a keen perception of present problems and needed solutions. Mr. Wells is a distinguished scholar and he is also a sophisticated realist in his understanding of the forces which are presently threatening our economic and political freedom.

Wendell Berge

Foreword

The problem of monopoly in America is essentially that of competitive accessibility to economic resources. The growth of monopoly in a country which is founded on the theory of free competition is significant in that it reveals the difficulties with which we are confronted in our attempts to control our social environment in the light of our theory of individual economic freedom. The discordance between our economic ideal and the reality of the growth of monopoly is the American manifestation of the difficulties inherent in man's attempts throughout history to solve the problem of the control of the social environment.

In accordance with this view a part of the present book is devoted to an analysis of the theories which have dealt with the question of social control, beginning with the early utopias, the theories of the Utopian socialists, the Marxian scientific socialism and ending with the social philosophy of the American democracy. Such an analysis is to serve the purpose of crystallizing those peculiarly American trends in our social life which are struggling to counteract the anti-social forces driving us towards the domination of our economy by concentrated economic power. This struggle constitutes a phase of the crucial problem of the age — that of the exercise of the national free will versus the fatalistic drive of historical determinism as formulated in the Marxian theory of historical materialism. Since it concerns the vital question of a democratic control of our social environment through the competitive accessibility to economic resources, the eventual outcome of the contest between these two social forces will determine the fate of this country as a democratic state — a state reaching towards the people's mastery of their own destiny.

The development of monopoly in America and the possible solution of this problem considered in the light of man's historical efforts to master his social environment are discussed in this book in terms of the dynamic operation of the law of causality. That this presents the only firm ground for the understanding of the social as well as the physical world, the author accepts as his thesis. As Professor Edward Hallett Carr points out, "Unless . . . we are content to believe that history has no meaning, we are bound to treat it as a coherent sequence in which one set of events or ideas leads on to another set of events or ideas and helps to influence and determine them . . ." What is true of history is true of the other social sciences. In recent times a number of distinguished physicists have questioned the validity of the law of causality in the realm of physics. A cursory summary of their views as well as that of Albert Einstein who holds to the concept of causation is contained in a note appended to Chapter II of this book.

Because of the impossibility of experimentation in the field of social relationships and our insufficient knowledge of the mainsprings of mass psychology as conditioning mass behavior, the identification of causal sequences in the evolution of social phenomena is an arduous task. This is complicated by the fact that with the development of more complex and intricate social relationships, social changes become more elusive to formulation in terms of the operation of the law of causality. As a result of the unforeseen social catastrophes of the recent decades which have revealed the inadequacy of the economic and social theories of whatever school of thought they were expressive of, history has begun to seem like a succession of fortuitous events. This would be true if social phenomena were taking place in a vacuum. But since they are imbedded in the reality of life, they obey of necessity the laws of causal sequences. As Hegel stated it, "whatever is real is rational"; in other words, whatever happens is the result of causal necessity.

The profound social and economic transmutations of recent decades have brought out in a vivid manner the significance of the law of causality as it determines social changes particularly with reference to the economic factor. It is to the extent that we can learn the lessons implied in these changes as they reflect the operation of the law of causality in its dynamic and cultural aspects and crystallize them in the light of our American ideals that we can hope to develop a basis for an effective democratic control of our social environment.

The author wishes to state that he is alone responsible for the ideas and statements contained in this book.

Henry A. Wells

CONTENTS

CHAPTER I

Monopoly As a Problem in the Control of the Social Environment

The problem of monopoly is almost as old as organized society. It appears throughout man's history in various forms, depending upon the determining factors of a given economic stage. In a feudal economy it assumes the form of control of land by feudal lords; in the present day industrial countries it manifests itself as private control of channels of trade, the means of industrial production, and financial facilities.

The problem of monopoly is essentially a question of whether there shall be suitable accessibility to economic resources. As such it serves as a common denominator of the various economic problems which, in one form or another, have agitated mankind since the beginning of organized society.

A nation lives off its economic resources. These comprise land and other natural resources, the means of production and the mechanism of distribution. The fact that the life of a nation depends upon these resources underlies all our economic problems, in whatever guise they appear.

Earnings and incomes are indexes of accessibility to economic resources. Low earnings in relation to the cost of commodities indicate a limited degree of accessibility to these resources. Conversely, the concentration of wealth and high incomes within a restricted group of the population points to limitations on opportunities of access to these resources. The gravity of the problem of monopoly lies in the fact that an equitable accessibility to economic resources, the source of life of a nation, is the condition *sine qua non* of the nation's welfare.

Competitive Theory and Monopolistic Practice

Within the last thirty years, as a consequence of the Russian Communist Revolution and of the ravages caused by the two World Wars, the problem of equitable accessibility to economic resources has appeared before the world in sharper outlines than ever. The Soviet Union is endeavoring to solve it through the nationalization of the means of production and distribution, interwoven with a revolutionary departure from the political theories of Western democracies. In Western Europe, the tendency, possibly concealed for the time being by the European Recovery Program, is towards the nationalization of

1

essential industries within the framework of democratic liberties, which may possibly be realized under the Labor Government in England.

The traditional concept of economics in the United States is expressed in the theory of the capitalism of free enterprise working under conditions of freedom of competition. Competition is conceived as a balancer of conflicting interests, leading to equitable opportunities of accessibility to economic resources. Monopoly capitalism, through interference with freedom of competition, places a barrier between economic resources and the great body of the economically weaker elements of the population.

Through the development of monopolistic combinations and practices, competition has to a considerable extent disappeared from our economic life. The problem of re-establishing competition through the return to the capitalism of free enterprise is assuming an importance even far beyond its economic significance. Against the background of the momentous world contest between collectivism and individualism the American idea of economic freedom becomes the symbol of the American way of life, that complex of social and ethical values which gives American democracy its distinctive character.

Within the American society a struggle is taking place between democracy as an expression of individualism and monopoly capitalism as a vehicle of nascent collectivism. That democracy has been losing ground in this struggle is indicated by the giant strides made by monopoly despite a strong anti-monopoly tradition which was intended to be enforced by the fifty year old Sherman Antitrust Act and subsequent anti-monopoly legislation. Through the concentration of economic power, monopoly capitalism is leading this country toward the situation which caused other countries to consider the nationalization of economic resources either through revolutions or through parliamentary reforms.

The contrast between the traditional American ideal of private enterprise working under competitive conditions and the growth of concentrated economic power is so conspicuous as to raise serious doubts concerning possibilities of the fullest development and fruition of our system of free enterprise. The enforcement of antitrust laws becomes a task of momentous importance. Considering the significance of competitive accessibility to economic resources, essential to a competitive economy, antitrust enforcement appears as a basic tool in the war waged by the forces of democracy against the growing threat of certain socio-economic theories which are alien to the spirit of American economics. Antitrust enforcement becomes a problem of reconciling reality with ideals; of counteracting the growth of monopoly capitalism by creating opportunities for the revival of the capitalism of free enterprise. It becomes a means through which the American people may master their social environment against the onslaught of blind antisocial forces of monopoly capitalism. These, if unchecked, could drive us, through the growing regimentation of economic life, towards some form of economic totalitarianism with adverse effects on our social ideals.

The possibility of a reconciliation of American reality with American ideals is weakened by the fact that the impact of monopoly on our social consciousness has been felt in varying degrees throughout the period of its growth. The harmful effects of the action of a socially destructive force must be sufficiently acute to give impetus to action. It is in this that the gravity of certain social problems lies. By the time the impact of an antisocial force is sufficiently strong to lead to an active realization of its significance, the social relationships affected are solidified to such a degree that a pragmatic solution of the problem involved, as contrasted with a radical one, presents considerable difficulties.

The history of the growing concentration of private economic power in this country presents a conspicuous example of how the possibilities of solution of a social problem lag behind the dynamics of social relationships. The first step undertaken to cope with economic concentration was made in 1890, when conditions developed in the American economy which began seriously to restrict competition through the absorption of business concerns by strong competitors. This step took the form of the passage of the Sherman Antitrust Act which in the succeeding years was complemented by other measures such as the establishment of the Federal Trade Commission and the passage of the Clayton Act. Neither of these measures was afforded sufficient opportunities of being enforced to prevent the development of concentrated private economic power. The Clayton Act, moreover, although found deficient with reference to its basic provision, was not amended until 1950 despite several legislative attempts to make it attain the purpose for which it was intended.

A law does not operate in a vacuum. It is a dead letter unless it finds adequate support among those groups of the population whose interests it purports to represent. In the case of the victims of monopolies, these groups comprise the mass of farmers, workers, and small business men, in other words, the overwhelming majority of the American people. Under a democratic social order which is supposed to guarantee the execution of the will of the people, the anti-monopoly laws, being the expression of the American tradition of free competition, should have prevented the encroachments of monopoly on our economy. If we hold that under a democratic regime the majority of the people have the power to order their lives as they see fit, through legislation enacted and enforced by the representative organs of government, the growth of monopoly would indicate that the laws which are designed to curb it have not had the proper support from the people at large.

From an American point of view the forces which led to the monopolistic domination of our economy are anti-social forces. But their impact on our life has apparently not been sufficiently strong or sufficiently overt in the past to arouse the American people to action in providing opportunities for an effective enforcement of the antitrust laws.

And yet what demand for action against monopoly there has been, has come from the grass roots. That its threat to our economic freedom was felt by the people as far back as the year 1890 is shown by the fact that the Sherman Antitrust Act was passed largely through the influence of organized farmers. The monopolistic activities of large industrial and business corporations looked ominous, too, at the time of the first great merger movement which took place soon after the passage of the Antitrust Act. "There were real grounds to fear that a few large corporations would soon control all the major industries of the United States with the consuming public considered only to the extent of what the traffic would bear by way of price exactions." [1]

That the Sherman Antitrust Act and the succeeding anti-monopoly measures had the continuous endorsement of the lower income groups of the American people is evident from the sensitiveness of political leaders to the monopoly problem. Our anti-monopoly tradition is popular with the masses of the people to such a degree that the political leadership finds it dangerous to disregard the issue of monopoly even if the word is seldom followed by the deed.

It is patent that the growth of monopoly has had a certain impact on the consciousness of the American masses. If it has not produced a determined counteraction, it is only because its impact was weakened by the play of environmental and physical factors distinctive to America. With respect to environment it should be noted that the American continent, even after the disappearance of the frontier, presented for a long time sufficient opportunities for expansion to attenuate the antisocial effects of the development of monopolies. Among the physical factors there were the soothing effects of the periods of illusory prosperity especially those which followed in the wake of the

World Wars. Even in the depression of the thirties, the temporary rehabilitation of our economic life consequent upon artificial injections and economic pump priming soon counteracted the first serious warning to America of the danger to our economy of a monopolistic control of our economic resources.

The essential factor in the failure in the past to arouse militant action against the progress of monopoly is that the periods during which the greatest business consolidations took place coincided with periods of prosperity. The depression of 1907 brought the first great merger movement to an end. The prosperity period of the twenties saw such a flowering of mergers that it is known as *the* period of mergers and consolidations. What this means in terms of the relation between impact and counteraction is that when an intensive monopolization takes place during a prosperous period the people at large feel too contented to be aroused to combat the evil of the ever-growing concentration of private economic power.

Monopoly Capitalism as a Stage Toward Collectivism

The steady march of monopoly may mean that there is an inexorable force at work which drives us toward the goal indicated by Marx — essentially the elimination of private competitive enterprise. The significance of this trend is being impressed forcibly on the consciousness of the thoughtful observers of the evolution of the American economy. It was given expression in an official report of the Federal Trade Commission to the 80th Congress of the United States. On the basis of an authoritative analysis of facts the Commission stated that "either this country is going down the road to collectivism or it must stand and fight for competition as the protector of all that is embodied in free enterprise." [2]

In the terms formulated by this report the problem of monopoly assumes a significance which it had not had until recent times. That significance became evident when the world was shaken by the Russian Revolution which, for the first time in history, abolished the right of private property in those economic resources which are the sources of life in society. Brought about was the socialization of the means of production and distribution. The theory which underlies these actions is based on a concept diametrically opposed to the American principle of competitive access to economic resources.

The social and economic changes that followed in the wake of the communist revolution in Russia, one of the two most powerful countries in the world, are of a far greater significance than the social transformations which took place in the past. The Great French

Revolution and other successful upheavals, whether revolutionary or peaceful, changed, in many instances, the political, social and economic structure of a particular nation, but they left intact the principle of private property. The Russian Revolution did away with that basic constituent of private property which concerns the private ownership of the means of production and distribution. It adopted the principle of collectivism as the basis of its economic structure. In spite of deviations conditioned by the peculiar historical circumstances under which the Russian Social Revolution took place, the Soviet Union expects through economic collectivism to attain the degree of productive capacity which is considered essential to the full realization of its Marxian ideal of a classless collectivized social order.

On the other hand, America is apparently determined to uphold the principle of free enterprise, freedom of competition and freedom of individual opportunity. But it finds itself in a paradoxical position. Private enterprise is giving ground to the seemingly irresistible drive of monopoly capitalism and is heavy with dire forebodings as to the ultimate fate of the institution of private property. The above quoted excerpt from the Federal Trade Commission's report shows that this trend seems to be fulfilling, to a degree that can be inferred, the Marxian forecast in the realm of American economics.

However, despite the fact that the Marxian forecast is proving plausible in our economics, the outlook on life and the mass psychology of the American people have not been formed in the mold envisaged by Karl Marx and the other theoreticians of Marxism. The forecast has definitely failed, so far, in its prognostications concerning the formation of a revolutionary state of mind through the elimination of the middle class and the proletarization of factory workers. The American people, including the industrial working classes, have preserved a pragmatic middle class outlook on life — whatever may be happening to the middle class as such — instead of acquiring under the influence of industrial centralization and concentration of economic power, a revolutionary psychology.

Under these conditions the attempt to solve the problem of monopoly embraces a wider range of considerations than the passing of suitable laws and providing the means for their enforcement. Legislation in a democratic country, that is, a country governed by the consent of the governed, is a means of controlling the social environment in accordance with the ideals of the nation. With respect to monopoly, which presents the most serious problem in the matter of American social control, there is harmony between the American social philosophy and the attitude of the majority, with reference to anti-monopoly legislation. This legislation contemplates the prosecution of monopolistic practices which restrict competitive access to economic resources. It is intended to give the people as a whole the means to control the relations between individuals, so as to afford an opportunity to share in economic resources in accordance with ability and industry. It is considered a method of social action to free the mass of the people — the farmers, labor, small business and consumers generally — from the relation of subservience to those groups who, either through the high-handed tactics of old or through the modern subtle and sophisticated methods, have acquired a monopolistic control over our resources.

The problem of monopoly appears as a basic constituent of the larger problem of the control of the social environment. As such, the possibilities of its solution are interwoven with the difficulties inherent in the nature of social as distinct from physical phenomena. These difficulties arise from the fact that man is an integral part of the environment over which he wants to exercise control; that social phenomena do not lend themselves to scientific experimentation and the testing of hypotheses; and, above all, that human relations which make up our social environment involve the consideration of mass behavior, a reflex of mass psychology, a branch of human knowledge of considerable elusiveness. That we have allowed monopoly to reach its present proportions means that we were thwarted in the past in our aspirations to control our social environment. This fact assumes a great significance since it concerns the vital problem of democratic accessibility to the sources of life of the nation.

Historical Attempts to Control the Social Environment

The problem of control of the social environment in a democracy is the problem of attainment of social and economic justice in the relations between the members of society. Until the advent of democracies in the advanced countries of the world, whatever social or economic justice was granted by absolute rulers was due to considerations of either profit or fear. Popular efforts to attain justice on a wide and fundamental basis were in the form of elemental upheavals, of revolutions which overthrew what appeared to be the foundations upon which the whole fabric of injustice seemed to rest. Revolutions are unconscious attempts to solve the problem of control of social environment. They could not have happened if they had not originated in despair, caused by discontent accumulated through years of oppression. They were not the result of reasoning but that of fatalistic historical forces which germinated in the interaction of oppression, deprivation and despair, to become an inexorable drive.

Attempts to consider the problem of control of social environment in a conscious and reasoning manner began with Plato's *Republic* which outlined the plan of an ideal society. This was followed, through succeeding centuries, by other plans of a utopian nature.

In the middle of the 19th century appeared the Marxian theory which was designated by its authors and followers as "scientific socialism" to set it apart from the utopian socialism of the early part of the century. The distinguishing characteristic of the Marxian theory is that its treatment of social problems is based upon the concept of the dynamic operation of the law of causality. The utopian schemes of an ideal society reflected a static point of view. The utopians were seemingly unaware of the significance of the action of historical forces as conditioning the possibility of a solution of social problems. This defect in their reasoning was largely responsible for their having failed to perceive the relation between the actual conditions of the epoch in which they lived and any possibility of a realization of their plans.

Marx developed his theory of the conditions which were to lead to a new social order through the study of the evolution of social relations in the light of his materialistic interpretation of Hegel's dialectical method. In accordance with this interpretation, the development of human society takes place not elementally and haphazardly but by necessary sequences of causes and effects operating through the resolution of contradictions. These sequences continue through three stages which develop in every society — the thesis, the antithesis and the synthesis — the synthesis being the realization of a new social order. "The result of development — the new in history — is prepared by the entire march of the old, of the previous stages, and the new comes to replace the old in accordance with an inner permanent requirement."[3]

In Marx's interpretation of this statement the new society will come into being with a sort of fatalism, through an explosive revolutionary outbreak which would liberate the nucleus of the new social order hidden within the old and formed through the historical development of society.

At the opposite pole from this theory stands democracy, especially the democracy of the American type. The theory which underlies the concept of social organization in our democracy has not been formulated with the explicitness of the Marxian theory. Its implications of a reasoned social action are, however, clearly perceived in the theories of Locke and the French encyclopedists of the 18th century, in the writings of the political leaders of the American Revolution, in the

Declaration of Independence and in the principles underlying our legislation and legislative procedure. The entire process of our law enactment bears witness to the endeavor to found legislation on a conscious and reasoning attitude toward the social environment such as implies the tacit acceptance of the significance of causal sequences. That the operation of causality is accepted in its dynamic aspect is borne out by the provision made for amending the Constitution. Constitutional amendments are based on recognition of the fact that social relationships change and that these amendments provide the opportunity for a conscious control of these changing relationships. This is true of those judicial interpretations which keep abreast with the progress of society. As Professor David Fellman points out:

". . . our Constitution is a living and changing instrument of government and . . . this explains its success. The history of the gradual expansion of the commerce clause to meet the needs of a changing civilization clearly illustrates the nature of American constitutional growth. It would be futile and pointless to inquire whether it was the 'intent' of the Founding Fathers to bring within the scope of the Federal commerce power the regulation of homegrown wheat consumed on the farm; the necessities of a market economy and intelligent judicial statesmanship have given us some twentieth century law for an economic society that could not have been anticipated in 1787. It is doubtful that the Founding Fathers thought of old-age insurance when they adopted the general welfare clause, but who will seriously quarrel with the decision that sustained its constitutionality." [4]

The concept of social movement is implied in our legislation. When the dynamics of causal relations led to the encroachment on freedom of competition by monopolistic combinations, the Sherman Antitrust Act was passed to meet this threat to economic freedom. The strategic position which was acquired by the railroads, for example, as a result of the expansion of economic activities on a national scale gave them the power to affect the vital interests of our population. They came to control transportation, which is one of the determining factors in the proper functioning of the national economy, and thus took on a public utility character. This was recognized in legislation regulating various aspects of the railroad problem, especially as they concern freight and passenger rates.

An effective functioning of the democratic machinery can be attained only through such adaptation of legislation to changing social relations in recognition of the dynamics of causal sequences. It aims at checking the action of antisocial forces. Otherwise, the accumulation of discontent caused by the discordance between legislation and the changing conditions of life would conceivably lead to a radical and even explosive solution of social problems. The development of monopoly in this country presents a conspicuous example of such a discordance in a field of activities shown to be of basic importance to the welfare of the country, inasmuch as it concerns the problem of access to economic resources.

Restrictive federal and state acts such as the "fair trade" laws combined with monopolistic practices are undermining our competitive system. This could develop into a situation in which even government regulation would be found insufficient, as it is already recognized to be with respect to railroads. The growth of monopolies is leading us toward the consideration of the possibility that the only means to harmonize legislation with changing economic conditions is through public ownership. Starting with what are recognized at present as public utilities, this might extend to other branches of our economy. Since, however, the feeling for a competitive economy is so strongly imbedded in the American psychology, the development of conditions leading to the idea of public ownership as the only possible solution of the problem of access to economic resources would confront the American people with a bewildering social dilemma; the significance of which would transcend the possibility of a pragmatic disentanglement of contradictory situations.

Democratic Efforts at Conscious Social Control Threatened by Monopoly

Consideration of various facts and principles leads to certain almost inevitable conclusions:

First, the well-being of a nation as a whole depends upon a proper utilization of economic resources;

Second, monopoly capitalism, through the isolation of economic resources, interferes with competitive accessibility to these resources and such interference violates the American principle of their democratic utilization;

Third, absence of competitive accessibility to economic resources makes a democratic country comparable to those agricultural nations in which concentration of land ownership has diverted the benefits to a handful of landowners and has deprived the mass of the people of the possibility of utilizing the land for the benefit of the nation. The conclusion to which we are forced is that the conquest of our economy by the forces of monopoly capitalism would ultimately lead to the same consequences that followed the monopolization of land in agricultural countries.

Distress is bound to appear sooner or later whenever a barrier is placed between the mass of the population and the economic resources of a country. This circumstance may ultimately lead to a change of even a democratic people's ideology toward some form of socialism. It accounts for the adoption of this idea by nations which, either through age-old oppression or through the disorganization consequent upon the end of the second World War, are mistrustful of the possibility of attaining a high level of economic stability through a democracy based on individual economic freedom. The relation between economics and ideology is impressing itself more and more on the thoughtful observers of our national life. This can be gathered from the following statement, representative of numerous similar pronouncements, made by Bishop Bernard I. Sheil of the Catholic Archdiocese of Chicago before the convention of the American Veterans' Committee: "People who are well-fed, well-clothed, and well-housed are not interested in communism. If we make American democracy work, not only politically, but economically and socially as well, we can conquer any ideology."[5]

Since there is a causal relation between economic conditions and the ideology of a people, it is obvious that the solution of a basic economic problem does not lie along the path of conjurations and incantations against theories which we consider as not in conformity with our way of life. It lies in our case along the path of conciliation of economics with democracy through the release of the forces of enlightened individualism as contrasted with the idea of "rugged" individualism. Enlightened individualism, compatible with the interests of society as a whole, constitutes the essence of the American social and economic philosophy.

Considered in its economic phases, the American concept of individualism is reflected in efforts to bring about competitive access to economic resources by freeing business enterprise from monopolistic restrictions. This is the practical utilitarian aspect of antitrust activities. However, as a result of the turmoil in which the world finds itself, consequent upon the spread of ideals of collectivism and socialism, the economic meaning of efforts to curb the power of monopoly merges into the wider social and historical aspects of the problem of concentration of economic power.

In these wide aspects, monopoly capitalism appears as an economic force which plays a double role. It thwarts the attainment of the American ideal of social freedom, which is interwoven with economic freedom. It becomes, also, a powerful tool in this country of the fatalistic forces of history, mentioned above, which have already brought about radical changes elsewhere. By their working through despair generated by age-old oppression and postwar economics, disaster, and social demoralization, these forces are driving many nations of the world either to actual experiments with, or to earnest consideration of, theories of social organization which profess to point the way to a full life through the merging of the individual in the collective.

In its report to the House Small Business Committee the Federal Trade Commission calls attention to the threat of monopoly to political freedom. "In the opinion of the Commission," says the report, "the present and still growing concentration of economic power in the United States constitutes today's greatest domestic challenge to the American theory of competitive enterprise, and, along with it, all that is embodied in the meaning of the somewhat intangible, but nonetheless real, meaning of 'the American way of life' and 'freedom of economic enterprise.' . . . Large corporate consolidations make cooperation within each industry or trade group easier and lead inevitably to cartel organizations in America as well as in Europe. . . . We do not have to wait years (when it may be too late to take corrective action) for a political demonstration of the effects of cartelization on our economic and political life. The experience in Europe, which will be repeated here if monopoly is not adequately controlled, is spread on the record for all to see. The story of the super government of I. G. Farben is a good example of what can happen here. Also, private super government in industry leads almost inevitably to political super government." [6]

If we permit the power in governmental affairs to be placed in the hands of the few "we shall suffer the same penalties that we suffer if we permit the power in governmental affairs to be placed in the hands of a few people." [7]

Monopoly capitalism, through the elimination of competitive enterprises and the concentration of the economy of the country in private corporations, is bound to lead to a regimentation of our economic activities, to domination of the national life by private interests and to the impairment of political freedom.

Democratic Control and the Social Climate

The solution of a social problem, in organized society, operates through legislation. In a country under an absolute political regime the process of legislating is personal through the enactment of laws that are, in effect, decrees of the head of the state. In a democracy legislation is supposed to be the expression of the will of the people. The difference between the two kinds of legislation reflects the difference of the two kinds of regime in relation to the social environment. The power of legislation through the will of one person or a group of persons representing special interests is the carrier of those forces which lead fatalistically to revolutionary upheavals. For a revolution is the result of the grinding of man by the social environment and constitutes an effort to regain control of this environment. Legislation through consent of the governed is bent upon carrying out the ideals of the majority in a given social aggregate. It involves a continuous and gradual improvement of the social organism. It thus prevents the intensification of oppressive practices and the accumulation of mass discontent which drive nations to revolutionary attempts at the solution of social problems. It implies a determination to control the social environment in accordance with the will of the majority.

The economic power of vested monopolistic interests, which leads unavoidably to political power, is threatening to become the instrument of historical fatality to the same extent as the political power of the old-time absolute ruler who was the instrument by means of which the policies of landowning and other interests were carried out. Legislation and law enforcement are the focal points upon which is concentrated the action of the fatalistic forces taking the form of pressures exerted on government activities. These forces, if not counteracted, nullify the possibilities of an evolutionary economic progress.

The antisocial factor of which these forces are the outward manifestations is the misuse of the profit motive. The profit motive, which is supposed to play in a competitive economy the role of a carrier of economic freedom, is being misused to such an extent that it could convert our economy into an economic totalitarianism.

The intensity with which the misuse of the profit motive is carried on increases in proportion to growth of concentration of economic power. The lure of unrestrained profits leads to the domination of production and of markets; it influences legislation, prevents the enactment of measures which would strengthen the anti-monopoly laws, and weakens law enforcement. Its pressure is bearing down on every social and economic activity, and especially on those activities which come into being either to counteract the development of monopolies or to weaken their pressure on society.

Under conditions attendant upon a monopolistic environment in which the misuse of the profit motive determines economic relationships, the problem of monopoly cannot be solved within the framework of a blueprint or a schematic design. Its solution involves the consideration of a suitable climate; of an atmosphere congenial to our endeavors to solve the social problems with which we are confronted.

But considering the intensity of the drive toward the concentration of economic power, an expectation of prospects for a more sympathetic climate, making possible a pragmatic solution of this problem, would seem fantastic. The outlook would be gloomy indeed, were it not for a certain relation between impact and counteraction which has been peculiar to American democracy.

Impact generates a corresponding counteraction, the forms and intensity of which vary with the historical antecedents of a nation. In Russia the counteraction took the form of a violent overthrow of government, caused by a revolutionary energy accumulated through centuries of oppression. In democratic America, with the tradition of freedom as its historical background, counteraction to the impact of antisocial forces usually takes the form of legislation — a legislation which should embody the consciousness of social purpose interwoven with the concept of enlightened individualism.

The counteraction to the impact of the depression of the thirties resulted in a series of enactments of the socalled social purpose legislation exemplified by the Social Security and the Tennessee Valley Authority Acts and the intensification of antitrust activities. The progress of the idea of social purpose as affecting our social and economic relationships continued with undiminished strength even after the depression, notwithstanding the presumption that under generally favorable economic conditions there would be less incentive towards a critical attitude towards the social environment.

Despite occasional setbacks a social atmosphere was being formed in this country until the beginning of the hostilities in Korea which was developing an earnest public support for the enactment and adequate enforcement of legislation founded on the concept of enlightened individualism which has its mainsprings in the Declaration of Independence and the Constitution of the United States as embodying the formulation of the traditional American aspiration towards the fusion of social welfare with individual rights. This development held out a great promise for our democracy. It is only under conditions evolved through a congenial social atmosphere that a democratic nation is afforded wide opportunities to control its social environment and to counteract through democratic processes the action of the fatalistic forces which, through the collectivism of monopoly capitalism, are driving us to the reign of socialist collectivism.

The developing military economy threatens to open the floodgates to an intensive action of these forces. As in the case of World War II we are threatened with a further growth in the concentration of economic power. The momentous problem is to find means to reconcile the requirements of a war economy with the principle of free enterprise and to prevent the emergence of a completely centralized economy which may prove to be a prelude to some form of socialization of our economic life.

[1] George P. Comer, "Price Leadership", in *The Sherman Anti-Trust Act And Its Enforcement*, Winter, 1940, issue of *Law and Contemporary Problems*, Durham, N. C., Duke University Law School, p. 61.

[2] *Report of the Federal Trade Commission on the Merger Movement*, Washington, 1948, p. 69.

[3] G. F. Alexandrov, B. B. Bykhovskii, and others, *Istoriia Filosofii* (History of Philosophy), Vol. 3, Moscow, 1943, p. 277.

[4] David Fellman, "Separation of Church and State in the United States: A Summary View", *Wisconsin Law Review*, May, 1950, pp. 428-429.

[5] From the address of Bishop Bernard I. Sheil to the annual convention of the American Veterans' Committee in June 1947 as reported by the *Chicago Sun*.

[6] Statement by the Federal Trade Commission on July 1, 1946, to the House Small Business Committee quoted in the Commission's report to Congress on *The Present Trend of Corporate Mergers and Acquisitions*, Washington, 1947, p. 23.

[7] Statement of Tom C. Clark, Associate Justice of the Supreme Court of the United States, former U. S. Assistant Attorney General, before Subcommittee on Study of Monopoly Power of the Committee on the Judiciary, House of Representatives, 81st Congress, Serial No. 14, Part I.

CHAPTER II

Control of Environment — Physical and Social

Man's economic activities under whatever form they appear are the expression of the struggle with nature. Whether in primitive communities or in the present highly complex economic organization of society, his purpose is to obtain means of subsistence. In primitive communities it is a direct struggle. As society progresses, the direct struggle is complemented by an indirect struggle in the form of manufacture and industry. Agriculture, mining, manufacturing, transportation, distribution and even the production of luxuries are all varied forms of the struggle with nature. In this struggle man is confronted with the task of controlling physical forces and utilizing them to his own end.

Man is a paradox. His material existence is subordinated to the law of causality, which determines the sequence of material phenomena in virtue of which a given effect always follows a given cause. If a man is struck by a sufficiently heavy blow, he dies. If he goes without food for any length of time, he starves to death. The law of causality acts in his case with the same inevitability as it does in the physical world which surrounds him. On the other hand, the instinct of self-preservation leads him to oppose that very nature whose forces shape and determine his existence.

Man is placed in the apparently paradoxical situation of being, at one and the same time, a free and a non-free agent. He is a non-free agent to the extent that he cannot change the action of the law of causality to which he is subject with the rest of the universe. But that he does play the role of a free agent is attested by the results of technological advances which have enabled man to liberate himself from a complete subservience to nature.

By applying a lever a man with his bare hands can lift a heavy stone. The action of the lever is based on the principle that the greater the difference of distances between the stone and the support on one hand, and between the support and the arm on the other, the greater the ease with which the stone will be lifted.

When the stone is lifted by applying the lever, the law of causality has not been changed but has been confirmed. This law has been placed under conditions which make it act so as to produce the desired effect. Even in the absence of the possibility for man's chang-

16

ing the law of causality, the experiment with the lever explains, by analogy, the effects of the great technological accomplishments in subjecting physical laws to the will of man.

Francis Bacon, writing over three hundred years ago, expressed his confidence that nothing was impossible for man, provided that he hit upon the right key to nature's secrets. "I accept it" (i.e. nature), said he, "but only as raw material. We will listen to nature, but only that we may learn what language she understands. We stoop to conquer." [1]

The object of technology is to devise means to enable society to wrest from nature — in other words, to produce — the goods which contribute to a secure, comfortable and healthy material life. What is known as "pure" science underlying technology concerns itself with the possibilities of a systematic control of the action of the law of causality for purposes of production. Although the progress of technology may be hindered or facilitated by considerations of profit, it depends intrinsically upon accumulation of knowledge and upon the presence of talent and inventiveness.

In the technological phase of man's struggle with nature, the problem of man as a free and non-free agent has been solved. He has wrested from nature many of its secrets and has utilized them for his own purposes. He has obtained a measure of control over his physical environment by recognizing his own limitations. He has studied the principles which determine the action of physical forces, not for the impossible task of changing the laws governing the causal sequences of physical phenomena, but to place them under conditions under which they will act to attain a desired goal. His further progress in this field is dependent almost solely upon a still greater accumulation of facts concerning the action of the law of causality in its various manifestations.

Thus, man's freedom of action with reference to his physical environment is conditioned by his taking into consideration the inevitability of causal relationships. But in his struggle with nature, he is not concerned solely with physical environment. Serious complications arise, due to the fact that this struggle is carried on (in the form of production) through the social medium and, therefore, its effectiveness is determined by the peculiarities of the social structure as they affect social and economic relations.

Limitation of production has so far been one of the central problems in man's struggle with nature. In France, before the Great Revolution, feudal oppression had had an adverse influence on agricultural production. In modern industrial society, monopolization and cartelization react negatively on the volume of production by subordinating production policies to a consideration of profits through the domination of markets. Private interests, even today, prevent a full realization of what should be the social purpose of scientific research; namely, the fullest possible production of goods. And yet, the question of full production is crucial, interwoven as it is with the problem of a fair and equitable apportionment of the national income.

After centuries of social and economic development we still seem to be far from having attained a social system which can insure all the members of society an opportunity to share equitably in the continually increasing means of subsistence and material comfort which we are wresting from nature. After decades of a tremendous amount of study and research, we are confronted with an avalanche of contradictory and mutually exclusive views concerning our economic problems. These conditions reveal the extent of the uncertainty and bewilderment which we experience in our attempts to control our social environment.

Thus, although the paradox of man as both a free and non-free agent has been solved in the realm of physical phenomena, that paradox has not been solved in the domain of social relationships. Most of our economic thinking shows, however, our acceptance of the theory that the law of causality operates in the social world as well as in the physical universe. It shows, also, our feeling that knowledge of the law's operation would enable us to use it for the purpose of controlling our social environment. Thus, when we are confronted with a social and economic evil, if we say that such and such a measure will eliminate it, we admit the working of the law of causality. We say, in fact, that if we do such and such a thing, such and such an effect will follow. If we did not accept this thought in the life and development of human society, we would have to give up all hope of a conscious change in social relationships. But because we do accept it, hope of such change persists.

The urge to find a way out of the labyrinth of interactions and mutual influences in the realm of social relationships through the study of the laws of causal sequences has led to the formulation of theories which assign to some one factor a determining causal influence on the entire range of social phenomena. Idealistic theories ascribe a decisive role to the idealistic factor, to ideas as motive forces of social changes; other theories consider the political factor as having a determining influence on the life of society; during the past century Karl Marx and Frederic Engels elaborated a theory (known as Marxism) which places emphasis on economics as the impelling factor of all social action.

The insufficiency of deterministic concepts becomes especially obvious in connection with the socio-political developments which took place within recent decades in this country and abroad. As will be shown in a subsequent chapter, the significance of the economic factor as a corrective of a purely political democracy was brought to our consciousness by the depression of the thirties combined with developments in other countries. Not only was it brought out more strikingly than it could have been by research and study but it compelled us to vigorous economic action which no amount of theoretical studies could initiate. On the other hand, the validity of the Marxian concept of the deterministic role of economics in the life of society was undermined by the history of the labor movement in the Western World and by the difficulties which the Soviet government experiences in its efforts to implant collectivism in the economy of the Soviet Union. These difficulties are due to the strength of factors of an idealistic nature—inherited psychical characteristics.

While the search for a determining all pervading cause is bound to be fruitless, it played a salutary role as a searchlight which revealed causal sequences within the evolution of social phenomena. As society progresses, as its life undergoes changes, we obtain more and more information as to the operation of the law of causality in social relationships. This enables us to act with a greater understanding without, however, ever hoping to arrive at perfection in social action which depends upon an unattainable, complete and exhaustive knowledge of the relative validity of the action of the various factors which determine social phenomena.

We will probably never obtain a truly comprehensive understanding of the laws governing the sequence of social phenomena. But an analysis of experiments undertaken in the past together with a study of the trends which are being revealed at the present momentous period in the history of civilization, should be of great significance in guiding us along the path of progress toward social control.

Doubts as to the validity of the law of causal necessity in its application to social phenomena arise in most cases from a mechanistic concept of its operation — a concept which does not take account of the complexity of the phenomena which are considered. There is a difference between the action of this law in the realm of physics and the much more complicated mode of its operation in the field of social relationships, where as Schopenhauer points out, the *motive* determines causal necessity.

In Schopenhauer's view there exists a *fourfold* necessity, in conformity with the *four* forms of the Principle of Sufficient Reason — the logical, physical, mathematical and moral necessity. He defines physical necessity as one "in virtue of which, as soon as the cause presents itself, the effect must infallibly follow."[2] Moral necessity which rules in the realm of social phenomena is described as one "in virtue of which, every human being, every animal even, is *compelled*, as soon as a motive presents itself, to do that which alone is in accordance with the inborn and immutable character of the individual. This action now follows its cause therefore as infallibly as every other effect, though it is less easy here to predict what that effect will be than in other cases, because of the difficulty we have in fathoming and completely knowing the individual empirical character and its allotted sphere of knowledge, which is indeed a very different thing from ascertaining the chemical properties of a neutral salt and predicting its reaction."[3]

Motive is conditioned by a variety of factors both of an economic and cultural nature. As civilization advances motive becomes synonymous with purpose.

As with an individual, so with society, progress in the direction of a goal, even without the prospects of attaining it, may lead towards a maximum possible happiness, both spiritual and material. But to render progress fruitful we must be guided by a definite aim. The *problem* of control must be subordinated to the *purpose* of control.

From this point of view the problem of social control is fundamentally different from that of the control of the physical environment. In the case of the latter, our purpose is to obtain from nature the maximum of goods, products and services to insure the basis for the material well-being of society. The means by which we obtain these are common to all nations. Whether in a communist or a capitalist society, we use in our struggle with nature the same scientific principles and the same technological devices. From the technical point of view, science and technology are as efficient in a capitalist as in a communist state, and as they were in the former totalitarian Germany. But because of national characteristics and physical differences, this effectiveness varies, as between nations, with respect to social control. For to be effective, the mode of action leading towards the control of the social environment must be in conformity with our state of mind and our social ideals.

We are frequently told that American life is undergoing a fundamental change; that free enterprise has practically disappeared as a result of the tremendous development of economic power in the form of cartels and monopolies; that the old is gone, never to return. We are told that we are drifting towards a social organization which will involve motif patterns of a nature different from those which have determined our historical development; in short, that we are faced with the possibility of an economic revolution.

Pessimistic intellectual reactions of this kind are not new in the history of mankind. But in the past whenever thoughtful and sensitive men have been confronted with the consequences of economic maladjustments, they have directed their thoughts towards the possibility of reorganizing their social environment. The search for a way out of these maladjustments has taken, for the most part, the form of utopian schemes for creating a perfect society, and has reflected the concepts of social control considered as leading to the realization of their particular social ideal. An analysis of such schemes should prove of value if it bears on that basic problem in social control which concerns the question *not of what should be done* but of *what can be done* under circumstances conditioned by historical growth and by the state of mind of a particular social aggregate at a given period of social development.[4]

[1] Joyce O. Hertzler, *The History of Utopian Thought*, Macmillan, 1923, p. 148.

[2] Arthur Schopenhauer, *On the Fourfold Root of the Principle of Sufficient Reason and on the Will in Nature*, London, George Bell and Sons, 1897, p. 182.

[3] *Ibid.*, p. 182.

[4] The validity of the concept of causation is challenged by authoritative voices in the realm of physical sciences. A comprehensive challenge to the theory of causality is contained in a recently published book entitled *Albert Einstein, Philosopher-Scientist*, edited by Paul A. Schlipp, Library of Living Philosophers, Evanston, Illinois, 1949. It is a symposium dedicated to Einstein and containing twenty-five articles by distinguished scientists analyzing and appraising his contributions to science and to philosophical thinking. It is admitted that Einstein's work has set going an intellectual revolution which is probably greater than that of Darwin and which, outside of science as within it, can be compared with Hobbes' and Newton's three hundred years ago.

Most of the scientists who contributed to this symposium question the validity of the theory of causation on the ground that Einstein's own work in quantum physics leads to disbelief in an assured and rigid sequence of cause and effect. In his own contribution to this book Einstein takes issue with this view and holds to the concept of a rigid causal theory. In a letter to Professor Max Born, dated November 7, 1944, Einstein states: "I [believe] in perfect laws in the world of things existing as real objects, which I try to grasp in a widely speculative way." (page 176). And further, "It is [in this sense] that the theory of relativity maintains the reality of space and time. These conceptual systems describe relations holding between physical objects, namely, solid bodies, light rays, and watches. In addition, these relations formulate physical laws of great generality, determining some fundamental features of the physical world. Space and time have as much reality as, say, . . . the Newtonian forces of attraction." (page 302)

Max Born says, "Einstein himself was—and still is—convinced that there are structural properties in the excited atom which determine the exact moment of emission, and that probability is called in only because of our incomplete knowledge of the pre-history of the atom." (page 173)

CHAPTER III

Attempts to Create Utopias

In the evolution of human efforts to control the social environment, utopian thought occupies a place of considerable importance. The utopian thinkers sought to contend with conditions which were developing in consequence of the breaking up, first, of the patriarchal, and, later, of the feudal system. Their thoughts reveal a penetrating insight into the problem of the social contradictions of their times. But the impracticability of their theories shows that they were unaware of the action of social forces which condition the efficacy of theoretical speculations.

Ancient Greece

The first known attempt to work out a plan of an ideally conceived social organization dates to the time of the city-states of Ancient Greece. As a result of the development of commerce and of colonial enterprise, the tribal structure had begun to disintegrate under the impact of the new forces of individualism. Economic groups unknown to the tribal system had made their appearance — merchants, small manufacturing entrepreneurs, and the Demos. Economic and political problems had arisen, mostly in connection with the precarious situation of the Demos, that part of the population consisting of free workers who could not find remunerative employment because of the labor of the slaves. It was at that time that there appeared the first work delineating a plan of an ideally organized society, Plato's *Republic*. The full significance of this work can be realized only if we relate it to the position of its author in Greek Society, and to the characteristics of the philosophy of Ancient Greece.

The distinctive mark of this philosophy was the application of reason mixed with metaphysics to the analysis of the phenomena of the universe — in contrast to all former interpretations in terms of the action of supernatural forces. Many of the teachings of the various schools of Greek philosophy, which found their synthesis in Aristotle, laid the foundation for the disciplined thinking which has culminated in the science of today.

Combined with the habit of intellectual exploration of the world was the essentially Greek longing for harmony and justice. The Greek idea of justice is inherent in the concept of harmony, and the peculiar form in which justice appealed to the ancient Greek was bound in with his longing for harmony. Harmony, and its highest expression, beauty, was dear to the Greek heart. Any discordant note, whether in life, art or literature, was repulsive; it was equivalent to the Christian concept of sin.

Consequently, when, as a result of the breaking up of the tribal system, the thoughts of the Greek philosophers turned towards examining social phenomena, the first thing that struck their observation was the contrast between the well-ordered, harmonious tribal arrangement and the chaotic spectacle presented by the nascent individualistic society. Plato's vision of an ideal society reflects his Greek philosopher's yearning for the rule of reason but it is also influenced by his position as a member of the Greek aristocracy.

Plato's *Republic* was to be a social and political system administered by a caste of men — the teachers and rulers. These men from their very birth, were to be segregated from the rest of society to make them free from the influence of personal interest that might sway their judgment. The rulers were to have no personal property but were to live under conditions of common ownership of their means of subsistence. They were to be trained in philosophy, so that they might rule over their fellow men according to the dictates of reason.

The new society was to realize the ideal of harmony through a static and hierarchically ordered system in which the status of the individual was determined by the group or class to which he was born. The first class was, of course, the rulers. The second class consisted of officials, guardians and warriors, whose supreme virtue was to be valor or fortitude. Their duty was to maintain order, within and without the state. A third class was made up of the great mass of people, the manual laborers; these as farmers, artisans and tradesmen were supposed to provide by their labor and industry the external means of the state. "When each class does its duty and maintains its appropriate virtues the nature of the state corresponds to the ideal of justice and happiness. Justice, then, is social coordination, and the consequent harmony of the whole — a harmony effected because every individual is doing his work in the station of life to which he is called by his capacities." [1] To avoid friction, to work toward justice, and to preserve harmony, the power of accumulating money was to be circumscribed. This measure would eliminate the frequent manifestations of discontent caused by what Plato calls "the envy and the cupidity of the Demos", aroused by the sight of newly arisen plutocrats enriched by colonial enterprise. Elimination of the possibility of accumulating riches, together with the rule of reason by the teachers and philosophers, and a strict delineation of social classes were the principles laid down as being fundamental. They would lead to a society embodying the ideal of harmony, preserving and consolidating the social status quo, and eliminating the dangers of despotism as well as those of extreme democracy.

The Early Merchant Capitalism:
the Period of the Renaissance

The next great work which embodied the scheme of an ideal social organization was Sir Thomas More's Utopia. It was written in the years 1515-1516, at a time marked by the intellectual awakening of the Renaissance and the resurgence of humanism. It is permeated with the humanistic outlook on life and constitutes a reaction against the misery, injustice and discontent which followed the early stages of the development of merchant capitalism known in economic history as *mercantilism*. It was the period in the history of several European countries when the rigidity of the feudal class structure began to be undermined by the appearance on the historical stage of a class of merchant capitalists, by the building up of money fortunes, and by the growth of an urban middle class.

Like the disruptions of the tribal system in ancient Greece, the upsetting of feudal economy in England resulted in the uprooting of large numbers of people from the economic life of society as their former occupations were eliminated. A case in point is the notorious practice of "enclosures" occasioned by the mercantilist export policies. England, at the time, found a great foreign market for its wool, notably in the textile industry in Flanders. Raising sheep became more profitable than tilling the soil. Pastures began, to a large extent, to replace tillage. Thousands of farm families were driven off their lands and the land was "enclosed" for the raising of sheep. This led to new mass sufferings only different in type from those caused by the feudal system. Under feudalism the masses had been oppressed; the peasant serfs in several European countries had staged occasional revolts, sometimes under the form of religious protests — in which demands were often voiced for the return to the practice of the humanistic concepts of early Christianity. But the land was the peasants' direct source of livelihood. They had been "fastened" to the land, but on the land they had had an occupation which at least had provided them with some subsistence. The practice of "enclosure" to permit commercial use of the land led to the accumulation of riches on one hand and to mass unemployment on the other. In the first book of his "Utopia" More gives voice to his indignation at the "corruption of the clergy, at the luxury of the nobility and the gentry, at the sufferings of the poor. . . ."[2]

In addition to the effect of enclosures, "a further instability and disorganization of industry was produced by *engrossing* and *forestalling*, prototypes of what we now call 'corners' and combinations. The rich bought sheep and sold again at high rates, and in holding the cattle or whatever the stock of goods was, the process resulted in much scarcity — all because of the accursed avarice of the few."[3]

In his attacks on the economic and social injustice of the England of his day, More also protested against the institution of property, particularly as he saw it administered. He expressed his conviction that till the idea of property is abolished, "there can be no equitable or just distribution of things, nor can the world be happily governed; for as long as that is maintained, the greatest and the far best part of mankind will be still oppressed with a load of cares and anxieties."[4]

In accordance with these views, the first basic principle in More's *Utopia* is the community of property. According to Hertzler, "More has in mind the abolition of class distinctions and the equality of all citizens before the law; consequently the abolition of private property and the establishment of common possession is the surest way of bringing about equality of claim and the abolition of crime."[5]

As a result of the community of property, More's Utopians have no use for money. "He shows that as money loses its value, men's fears, solicitudes, cares, labors, and watchings would all perish, for there would then be no frauds, thefts, contentions, seditions, or treacheries arising out of the desire for this 'root of all evil'. Men would be able to devote themselves to something higher and better."[6]

The significant feature of More's *Utopia* as contrasted with Plato's *Republic* is that More "was primarily thinking of how the state could be conducted to make for social welfare, and since the evils, as he saw them, were largely economic and industrial, the remedies he suggests are primarily those of eliminating industrial evils and the overthrow of harassing conventions."[7] Plato thought primarily of social peace — rather than of the evils which caused it to be disturbed — and identified it with order and harmony and maintaining the status quo.

More, with his humanistic Renaissance outlook on life, sought to render men happy through equality of access to the sources of material well-being. He looked *forward* into the future, and his *Utopia*, according to Hertzler, "played no small part in the social and scientific progress of the sixteenth and the following centuries."[8] Plato, on the other hand, both as embodying the Greek idea of justice through harmony and as a member of the slaveholding aristocratic class, was disturbed by the disorders and the restlessness of Athenian democracy. But, unlike More, for the remedy he looked *back* to the authoritarian principle of the patriarchal tribal system. His ideal society as envisioned in the *Republic* was to attain harmony, and therefore tranquility, through a rigid caste system; governed through reason, but patriarchally, nevertheless, by the Kings — philosophers. The latter, being deprived of wives and of the right of individual ownership of property, would thus renounce "the natural impulses toward one's individual concerns, in order that they might devote themselves entirely to the general weal"[9] and govern society solely on the basis of reason.

To More the first step in the direction of social control was the elimination of private property for all. To Plato only philosophers were capable of such renunciation and social control was entrusted to the enlightened judgment of philosophers, ruling over a state in which social and economic relationships were hardened and class strife consequently eliminated.

More, as a representative of the humanistic current of the Renaissance, laid emphasis on the recognition of equal social rights as conducive to social welfare. In contrast, Sir Francis Bacon of Verulam (1561-1626), the representative of the natural science trends of the period, held that the perfectibility of human society depended primarily not upon changes in the laws of property and other social reforms, but "on the progress of science and the regulation of human life by the scientific spirit."[10] The central theme of Bacon's utopian work *The New Atlantis* is that scientific method will lead man to perfect living. He sought to attain Utopia through the rebuilding of society in the light of knowledge and discovery.

Although Bacon attached great importance, in his utopian visualization, to certain social factors such as the family, his utopianism centers about the influence of science and knowledge as the strongest force in bringing about an ideal society. It is apparent that in Bacon's view, man's control of the physical environment was the real goal. By leading to the highest possible degree of material welfare, this would eliminate the problem of control of the social environment.

In Italy, where the advent of merchant capitalism led to conditions similar to those which obtained in England, there appeared in 1623 a utopian literary product of the Renaissance, *City of the Sun* by Thomas Campanella, a Calabrian monk. This utopian dream envisioned a new social order of enlightened equality under the rule of a "Chief Metaphysician" and his subordinates. The officials of this government were elective and were selected from an eligible list limited to those whose training in the arts and sciences made them most competent to rule. In the *City of the Sun* there was neither private property nor family, both of which Campanella considered as interfering with the individual's devotion to the state. To Campanella this type of communism meant that all the members of the community participated in all the benefits of the community, material and spiritual.

The equalitarian principle basic to life in the *City of the Sun* also forms the keynote of a number of utopian works which appeared in the 18th century as a reaction against the misery of the people and the general disintegration of French society in the period preceding the French Revolution. The most remarkable of these utopias, Morelly's *Basiliade*, is conceived in the spirit of nature, characteristic of the "period of enlightenment" in the history of French philosophy. In Morelly's commonwealth, all work according to their capacity and all are rewarded out of the common fund. Inequalities are discouraged, and the strong supplement the requirements of the weak.

Early Stages of Industrial Capitalism

The economic distress which appeared in the wake of the Industrial Revolution gave birth to a number of utopian works in the first half of the 19th century. One such is Etienne Cabet's *Voyage en Icarie*, the utopia of the modern proletariat, in which is broached the idea of economic planning and regulation. In his scheme industries and manufactures are public property and the executive regulates the production and consumption of commodities. There is neither property nor money, buying nor selling. All alike work for the community, which provides for their needs. Cabet's work is the first in a chain of socialist utopian schemes, the most widely known of which are those of Saint-Simon (or rather of his followers), Fourier and Robert Owen.

As we pass from the utopians of the 16th, 17th, and 18th centuries to the utopian socialists of the early part of the 19th century — namely, the Frenchmen Saint-Simon and Fourier and the Englishman, Robert Owen — we pass into a social environment which was in the process of being shaped by capitalism. The criticism of the utopian socialists is consequently directed at the social and economic effects of the capitalist mode of production. As critics of capitalism they had a predecessor in the French Swiss economist Simon de Sismondi. "But, whereas Sismondi sought to return to small-scale industry of the domestic type, and idealized the latter, the utopian socialists sought escape from the social and economic consequences of capitalism through the substitution of a peculiar type of socialism." [11]

The absence of an organizing principle Saint-Simon saw as the principal vice of capitalism. "Everything in it is disjointed and disunited. In production and distribution there reigns anarchy; economics and politics are separated from each other and both are separated from science."[12] Saint-Simon considered capitalism as a transitory period from feudalism to a future scientific industrial system. In the survival of certain feudal elements such as large landowners and usurers he saw the weakness and lack of vitality of the nascent capitalist society. He divided society into two classes: landed proprietors and industrialists; in the latter group he included all those who work, the manufacturers, merchants, bankers and workers. As capitalism developed, however, Saint-Simon changed his concept of real workers. In his last book, The New Christianity, written in the early twenties of the 19th century, he came out in behalf of the working class, i.e. the proletarians. He declared the emancipation of the working class as the ultimate aim of his aspirations. But he remained an opponent of class struggle by advocating voluntary obedience to a hierarchy of benevolent captains of industry, industrial leaders, capitalists and bankers. These were to be the administrators. Saint-Simon gave them "the executive power and the control of taxation and expenditure and by so doing he gave them real temporal power."[13] The spiritual power was left to the savants, aided by men of letters and art. In his later work the Système Industriel (1821) he withdrew the spiritual power from the savants and handed it over to "positive philosophers." In his New Christianity (1825) he said that "all should labor for the development, material, moral and intellectual of the class the most numerous and poorest . . ."[14] In his thoughts about the future industrial society he also advocated the abolition of privileges. His followers extended this doctrine to include the abolition of the greatest of all privileges, that of inheritance. By making the state the residuary legatee, they thought to have a short cut to socialism.

The other great French socialist, Fourier, in his criticism of capitalism concentrated mostly on the system of distribution. He considered the principal cause of all evils the decentralization and consequent lack of organization of production, which, in his belief, led to the domination of the merchants. According to him, an ideal social arrangement would result in a rational organization of production. "As a result of the insufficient development of the capitalism of his day, and the flowering of commercial speculation during the revolution and restoration, Fourier was impressed by the antagonistic interests of the producers and the merchants. In the producer group he includes both manufacturers and workers, as does Saint-Simon. But Saint-

Simon's grouping of workers and capitalists in one class is conditioned by his thesis that the capitalists are the managers of industry and the leaders of the workers. Fourier's reason for uniting these two groups in one class is that, in his belief, "they are both the object of the exploitation of the agents of the circulation of goods, namely, the merchants and bankers." [15]

To evaluate Fourier's scheme of an ideal social organization, it is necessary to take into consideration that "early in life he became impressed with the fact that the present organization of society was a disastrous failure and should be condemned as such. About him he saw lying, deceit, wastefulness, discord, maladjustment, so he early set to work to build up a social scheme to promote truth, honesty, economy of resources, and the development of our natural propensities." [16]

As we shall see, Fourier thought that "our natural propensities" were constructive and in the direction of the good of all. His scheme rested upon the concept of emotions or "passions" as the main springs of human action. "The great master passion 'uniteisme' meant for Fourier that all men were naturally inclined to club together in social groups and work together for mutual good, instead of fighting with one another under a system of competition. But in order to permit this to work itself out effectually the existing artificial social environment would first have to be condemned and abolished. The environment would have to be helpful. Therefore, Fourier provided such an ideal environment and called it a phalange or phalanx — an environment in which the passions, having perfectly free play, would combine harmoniously, operate to society's benefit and justify this ideal environment." [17] This social organization or social unit he made the framework of human society.

Briefly speaking, each phalanx or phalange was to be a combination of a suitable number of individuals, occupying buildings known as phalansteries, and inhabiting land a square league or so in extent. This area was to be worked in agriculture and industry by the united efforts of the whole community, acting under the direction of managers chosen by the people. Fourier hoped to adapt employment to the inclinations and capacity of the laborer. In the phalange no work would be monotonous, for all would do what they wanted to do, and all would quicken the energy of their exertions as each attempted to distinguish himself. In the main, Fourier favored a complicated system of payment in proportion to services. The share of each type of service in the communal dividend would vary directly with its importance in fostering harmony, and inversely with the pleasantness of the work.

"Fourier's plan was a recognition of the fact that social organization must group itself around the requirements of industrial life, and, still further, that industrial life must be subject to the desires of the individual human mind. Fourier thought that his theory of the passions combined with his principle of association was going to change the lot of the human race by satisfying the basic desires common to most men, and luring them on to perfection by the seductions of profit and pleasures." [18]

The conditions created in England by a capitalism that was developed further than it had been in France at the time of Saint-Simon and Fourier, led to a variety of utopian socialism which is identified with the name of a successful and wealthy manufacturer, humanist and social thinker, Robert Owen. The introduction of new mechanical devices had increased enormously the productive powers of England, but they had also brought with them poverty and hardship. Robert Owen, who began life as an apprentice in a cotton factory and in later years made a fortune, winning fame as one of the greatest captains of industry, turned his thoughts to the solution of the problem presented by the frightful living conditions and factory conditions of the English workers of his day. He suggested several measures of social reform, such as a national scheme of education. He held that the education of the rising generation on rational lines will, in the long run, lead to remodeling social institutions. He also advocated the establishment of a Labor Bureau "for the purpose of obtaining regular and accurate information relative to the value and demand for labor over the United Kingdom." [19] He considered it "the primary duty of any government that sincerely interests itself in the well-being of its subjects to provide perpetual employment of real national utility in which all who apply may be immediately occupied." [20] Among the minor reforms which he advocated were the regulation of liquor traffic, the reform and ultimate suppression of the Poor Laws, the purging of the Church of theological dogmas, and the founding of universal charity.

In 1817, following the disorganization of industry caused by the ending of the Great European Wars at the battle of Waterloo, Owen set out in search of a remedy for unemployment and misery. It was then that he proposed his Utopia. "He propounded his scheme of 'villages of unity and cooperation', in which the unemployed were to be collected together into self-supporting communities, where they would cooperate for their mutual benefit." [21] He left his work as director and co-proprietor of the New Lanark Mills to preach his ideal of a cooperative world. "He saw the world made up of villages, rid of the capitalist and free from the private property which was completely incompatible with social well-being, producing solely for the collective good. . . . Briefly stated, he recommended that the Trade Unions turn themselves into productive societies, or that colonies of workers should be formed on the cooperative principle." [22] These colonies or villages of cooperation, with populations varying from 500 to 2000 souls, were to furnish the favorable environment conducive to high standards of conduct. Owen held that man was essentially a healthy animal in body and mind, and that he was fundamentally good; what was necessary for his proper development was a fitting environment. "Owen's fundamental postulate was that the object of human society was to increase the happiness of each individual to the greatest extent practicable that is consistent with the greatest happiness of the whole." [23]

In 1824 Owen went to the United States. "Ostracized and rejected by the ruling classes, a stranger to the labor movement," [24] Owen decided to put his plan of a cooperative community into practice in America. "In 1825 he bought from a religious sect of German farmers, who lived communally, 30 acres of land with buildings. It is here that he began to organize a cooperative community, called 'New Harmony'." [25]

The economic basis of the first cooperative communes, including New Harmony, was to be agriculture; industry was given an auxiliary role. "However, it is not correct to contend, as some investigators do, that Owen's community cooperation was purely agrarian. Owen demanded the eradication of private property not only in land but in other sources and means of production. Having had considerable experience as a merchant and industrialist he understood that industry cannot serve as an original arena for 'experimental' communes. Industry works for extensive markets and depends upon them entirely; to isolate industry from markets means to destroy it. Agriculture is a different matter. It is true that agriculture in his day was already dependent upon market outlets, but in this field there were more postulates for the creation of more or less self-sufficient enterprises which would be made to demonstrate the possibility of building a cooperative commonwealth. Owen did not consider cooperative communes as his ultimate end, but thought of them as being charged with the task of laying the foundation of a communal reconstruction of society." [26] Owen spent on the commune of New Harmony around £40,000, comprising three-fourths of his fortune. The commune ended in complete failure, having been in existence only three years.

Although in the earlier stages of his activities Owen had had no direct dealings with workers, his ideas and his efforts did not remain without influence on the working class. In London, as well as in the provinces, a series of societies came into being which were organized on Owen's principles. "According to the press information of the time, there were in existence by 1830, three hundred cooperative societies in various parts of England. There also appeared many cooperative periodicals and newspapers published in the spirit of Owen's ideas." [27]

All this took place in England without the participation of the ideological inspirer of the movement, who was during that time preoccupied with his New Harmony and did not observe what was taking place at home. Only after failing in America and returning to England did Owen perceive that in his homeland there was prepared a new field for his activities. "He began to gravitate towards the trade union movement. He wanted to turn the trade unions into unions of producers for the organization of cooperative communes. He brought about the establishment of a cooperative organization, 'The Grand National Consolidated Traders' Union' with the aid of which he contemplated the reorganization of society. He also organized a sort of bank called the 'National Market for a Just Exchange of the Fruits of Labor." [28]

Anyone who had merchandise could bring it to the bank; "The latter, after expert appraisal, would issue in exchange for the merchandise 'labor money,' i.e., a receipt which designated the number of labor hours spent (or rather which should have been spent) on the production of delivered merchandise. The owner of the receipt was allowed to receive, on its presentation, other merchandise in the bank, the production of which had required an equal number of labor hours." [29]

Both the bank and the traders' union ended in utter failure because of unsurmountable difficulties connected with the task of conducting socialist industrial and business enterprises in a capitalist environment.

Analysis of the Utopian Schemes

From the point of view of control of social environment, the Utopians deserve particular attention because of their consciousness of the existence of social laws. The characteristic common to the utopias is belief in the principle that environment plays a determining role in the question of human happiness; that it is of decisive significance in social relationships. Thomas More, Campanella, and the French Utopian Socialists ascribed poverty, misery, crime and all other social evils to a wrong social environment. This was a tremendous step away from the old concept, in virtue of which man was considered as individually responsible for whatever befell him.

The relation between environment and human behavior is brought out in a masterful way in Fourier's teaching about the nature of man in which he developed his theory of passions (or what we now call instincts) and which is the foundation stone of his ideal society. Moreover, "in contrast to the moralists of his day who divided human passions into good and evil, Fourier brings out another thesis: all passions are good, but they become bad only because of a wrong social structure. Therefore, it is necessary to struggle not against passions, but against that social system which makes passions bad. . . . Fourier wants to build a society in which all the human passions would have expanse for their development." [30]

The principle of causality is admitted, whether consciously or not, in all the Utopian theorizations about the future. It is revealed in all the relationships between their belief that property (individually owned) is the root of all evil and their advocacy of a common ownership of property. It also shows itself in the importance which they attach to education as a potent force in shaping the social environment. The reason, however, that their lofty generalizations lacked elements of reality is that they failed to think of social relationships — and, by implication, of the law of causality — in their dynamic and cultural aspects.

The social environment is made up of social relationships the essence of which is fluidity and change. This makes the problem of determining the operation of the law of causality among them infinitely more complicated than that of the operation of causality among the mechanical relationships which make up the physical environment. The utopians failed to consider that lower social forms are replaced by higher, through the development of new social relationships, the seeds of which originate with the lower forms, and that this evolutionary (or, at times, revolutionary) process is complicated by the operation of the law of causality according to the action and inter-action of physical, psychical, biological and cultural factors.

It is interesting to note that, although Saint-Simon and Fourier were conscious of the dynamics of history, and even worked out theories of social development, they ignored the historical factor in their speculations about an ideal social structure. Fourier, for instance, was certain that his system of phalanxes would reorganize society at whatever time in history it might be put into practice. He proclaimed that "humanity lost fruitlessly thousands of years on a senseless struggle with nature" because it did not know about his system.

Since the utopians ignored in practice the dynamic — historic — factor in social relationships, they did not realize that their schemes, being out of tune with their surroundings, were doomed to failure. It was pointed out earlier that Robert Owen's "National Consolidated Traders' Union" and his "National Market for the Just Exchange of the Fruits of Labor" failed because of unsurmountable difficulties connected with the task of conducting socialist industrial and business enterprises in a capitalist environment. Owen's enterprises were based on the concept of production for use, and consequently they could not function in an environment whose basic feature was production for profit.

The outstanding fact is that the social theory of property which underlies implicitly the utopian visualizations of communal ownership had not roots in the consciousness of the masses. Large scale production was only developing. Production was still individualized to a large extent; and the actual producers, artisans and workers in domestic manufactures were not entirely disassociated from the products of their labor. Contrast this situation with our conditions of highly developed concentrated mass production, when thousands of workers produce goods through a collective or social effort. When the individual worker is not conscious of goods as having been produced by his own labor exclusively, the social theory of property has much wider opportunities for acceptance. It may be accepted, not in the crude form of communal ownership of property, but rather in the form of collective ownership of means of production; or in the less extreme form of the nationalization of basic industries; or in the free enterprise concept of antitrust laws and other measures which are the expression of the idea that the use of private property by some should not interfere with the enjoyment of the right of property by others. But at all events, in the days of the utopian thinkers the possibility of acceptance of a social theory of property was precluded by the absence of large concentrated industry.

Moreover, the schemes of the utopians were doomed to failure because they were ignorant of the significance of what Hertzler calls the spirit of protest for reform purposes. Hertzler points out that "as idealists they were great; but if they had been agitators as well as idealists they might have been greater. For quicker effects there must be propaganda and action along with the ideals." [31] Even if they had been aware of this obligation, however, the difficulties of the time would probably have been too great to overcome.

For example, "protest" means protest against existing conditions. But to whom should such protest have been directed? Naturally to the ruling classes; but these very classes were the beneficiaries of the conditions which led to dissatisfaction. Then, too, no organized effort was possible in those days. This was true for a number of reasons: such as the low level of education; the absence of rapid and efficient means of communications; and, in the case of urban industry, the still insufficient concentration of industry and consequently an insufficient concentration of labor which lessened opportunities for an understanding by the workers of their mutual problems. (The revolts of the agrarian population in ancient times and in the middle ages were not organized protests. They were elemental uprisings of serfs and slaves driven to desperation by misery and hardships. They either ended in failure or had a passing effect.) It is significant that in the later period of Robert Owen's activities, industrial and economic conditions in general developed far enough to lead to the formation of strong workers' organizations, and thus provided an organized force that could probably have set in motion an effective protest.

These organizations were strongly in favor of Owen's schemes, but against Owen's wishes they intended to use them for purposes of a militant class struggle. It will be recalled that the "Great National Traders' Union", established by Owen, which worked in conjunction with his "National Market (or bank) for the Exchange of the Fruits of Labor" was supposed to be both a professional union and an organization of producers. However, "the workers who entered the Traders' Union demanded leadership in the struggle for their interests. They also wanted to carry through Owen's ideas by means of that weapon which was the most accessible to them—strikes." [32] In the minds of the workers, the "Great National Traders' Union" was to serve as a sort of seed-bed for the organization of mass strikes. "Although Owen was at the time sympathetic to the idea of a strike, he counted more on propaganda than on the class struggle. The strike was to be, in his belief, the last act, so to speak, of an already accomplished dramatic internal overturn. He was dissatisfied with the rising strike waves and with the sharpening of the class struggle. Differences arose between him and his collaborators, who were closer to the working masses and were considerably under their influence. . . . The failure to compose these differences led to a cessation of Robert Owen's broad social activities. Gradually, Owenism turned exclusively into a moral teaching, and Owen's organization into sects which aimed at creating a new religion on the basis of a materialistic philosophy." [33]

Thus, in its ultimate phase, the intellectual utopian movement, which began with Plato, comes into contact with a new movement which follows a materialistic interpretation of Hegel's philosophy that "history is not the expression of a predetermined plan, but is the result of laws immanent in historical life itself."[34] This new movement lays claims to being scientific because it bases its philosophy on the concept of social development from lower to higher forms by means of the law of causality operating through class struggle. The movement is known as the materialistic expression of Hegelianism. As Hertzler points out, "when the doctrines of the Utopian Socialists became blended with Hegelianism they ceased to be 'utopian' and became 'scientific.' The Hegelian conception of evolution found in the writings of Karl Marx as early as 1848, marks the turning point in social theory."[35]

[1] Joyce O. Hertzler, *The History of Utopian Thought*, Macmillan, 1923, p. 104
[2] *Ibid.*, p. 130.   [7] *Ibid.*, p. 134.
[3] *Ibid.*, p. 132.   [8] *Ibid.*, p. 127.
[4] *Ibid.*, p. 132.   [9] *Ibid.*, p. 134.
[5] *Ibid.*, p. 134.   [10] *Ibid.*, p. 147.
[6] *Ibid.*, p. 136.
[11] D. L. Rosenberg, *Istoria Politicheskoi Economii* (History of Political Economy), p. 265.
[12] *Ibid.*, p. 274.
[13] Joyce O. Hertzler, *The History of Utopian Thought*, Macmillan, p. 194.
[14] *Ibid.*, p. 197.
[15] D. L. Rosenberg, *Istoria Politicheskoi Economii* (History of Political Economy), p. 285.
[16] Joyce O. Hertzler, *The History of Utopian Thought*, Macmillan, p. 198.
[17] *Ibid.*, p. 200.   [21] *Ibid.*, p. 219.
[18] *Ibid.*, p. 203.   [22] *Ibid.*, p. 219.
[19] *Ibid.*, p. 218.   [23] *Ibid.*, p. 215.
[20] *Ibid.*, p. 218.
[24] D. L. Rosenberg, *Istoria Politicheskoi Economii* (History of Political Economy), 1940, p. 305.
[25] *Ibid.*, p. 305.   [28] *Ibid.*, p. 307.
[26] *Ibid.*, p. 305.   [29] *Ibid.*, p. 307.
[27] *Ibid.*, p. 306.   [30] *Ibid.*, p. 282.
[31] Joyce O. Hertzler, *The History of Utopian Thought*, Macmillan, p. 306.
[32] D. L. Rosenberg, *Istoria Politicheskoi Economii* (History of Political Economy), 1940, p. 309.
[33] *Ibid.*, p. 309.
[34] Joyce O. Hertzler, *The History of Utopian Thought*, Macmillan, p. 311.
[35] *Ibid.*, p. 311.

CHAPTER IV

Scientific Socialism

The fact that Marxism, or as it is also known, scientific socialism, "marks" in the words of Professor Joyce O. Hertzler, a "new turning point in social theory" should in itself merit attention. It acquires added significance for the following reasons:

(1) Because of its claim that it offers a scientific explanation of social phenomena and a scientifically conditioned forecast as to the future course of social development;

(2) Because of the undoubted influence it has had on economic thought;

(3) Because of the political and economic discussions and struggles which it has provoked with reference to the validity of its theory;

(4) Because of the fact that the theory underlying this movement has been applied in actual life, in a country embracing one-sixth of the earth's surface, the Soviet Union, with auxiliary deviations necessitated by the peculiar conditions under which the social revolution in that country took place;

(5) Because of the fact that the Marxian theory constitutes the battleground, in the Western European countries and elsewhere, upon which a struggle for supremacy is taking place between capitalism, on one hand, and communism and diluted Marxism, on the other; and the fact that this struggle lies at the root of all future peace in the world.

The Breeding Ground of Marxism

The 19th century, which witnessed the birth of Marxism, was characterized by an unprecedented flowering of thought in all the branches of human knowledge. In the humanities and in science, respectively, the towering figures of Hegel and Darwin represent the synthesis of the advancing thought of previous ages.

The philosophical reasoning concerning the surrounding world, which began with the philosophers of Ancient Greece, reached in the 19th century the synthetic phase of intellectual growth. Through Hegel, this has revolutionized the study of the humanities by introducing the concept of unity and necessity in the development of human relationships. Through Darwin it has led to the formulation of the law of development of the organic world. It was also during the 19th century that momentous changes occurred in the domain of technology which have industrialized the economic life of advanced countries and have consequently led to the formation of a large class uniform in status and deprived of the means of production — the industrial proletariat.

In this historical atmosphere, born from the coming-of-age of science and philosophy, and from the industrialization of society the Marxian movement arose. This movement was founded on the first comprehensive attempt to analyze historical and social phenomena by tracing the dynamic operation of the law of causality. The philosophical formulation of the movement has its roots in the Hegelian philosophy, stripped of its metaphysical concept of history as developing through the action of an "absolute idea" supposed to have existed prior to the appearance of man and nature. The development of this "absolute idea" is conceived by Hegel as a dialectical process of movement and change through the resolving of contradictions which arise in the course of the evolution of nature and society.

Dialectical Philosophy

The concept of dialectics originated in the reasoning of the philosophers of Ancient Greece, who understood by it the art of arriving at the truth by uncovering contradictions in the reasoning of the opponent and overcoming these contradictions. Later, dialectics became interwoven with the teaching of the idea of universal interconnection and development. Dialectics envisages all phenomena as dynamic, as eternally moving and changing. It considers the development of nature to be the consequence of the development of, and struggle between, contradictions in nature. The Greek philosopher, Heraclitus, taught that everything exists and at the same time does not exist; that everything flows and continually changes, arises and disappears. Another, the most outstanding philosopher of ancient Greece, Aristotle, investigated the essential forms of dialectical thought. But Greek philosophy, looking upon nature as a whole, did not reach the stage of quantitative exploration of the phenomena of nature without which the general dynamic picture of the world cannot become clear. Science was in its infancy and it was only in the second half of the 18th century that the dynamic concept of nature was scientifically analyzed in Kant's formulation of the theory of the historical formation of the solar system. In the philosophy of Hegel, however, dialectical historical thinking came to fruition.

Kant began his career by resolving the stable solar system of Newton and its eternal permanence — after the famous initial impulse had once been given — into a historical process: "the formation of the sun and of all the planets out of a rotating nebulous mass."[1] History began to be conceived as a process; as in constant motion, change, transformation and development. The source of self-movement and self-development was to be found in the contradictions of this process.

It is the dialectical concept of development, development through the resolution of contradictions, that constitutes the contribution of Hegel to dialectical thinking. "Even before Hegel it was dimly realized that all human existence is a unified process in which the concrete events, which are the subject of written history, are but incidental features; but this dim idea was not strong enough to color social thought; it had not yet reached the stage where it gave hope. It was merely a gestating principle. These nebulous conceptions were finally given form in Hegel's famous Lectures on the Philosophy of History and in the works of other 19th century philosophers."[2] History in Hegel's view of it was not the expression of a predetermined plan, but "the result of unfolding of the human spirit-cycle, repeating itself in different ways and in different ages with a sort of inherent capacity for self-development."[3]

Here may be perceived the reason for the influence of Hegel's concept of history on modern thought; it avoided the mistake of the utopians who considered that their visionary schemes could be put into practice regardless of time, simply through the efforts of men of good will. Hegelian philosophy explained the forward march of civilization by introducing into history the concept of necessity implied in the dynamic operation of the law of causality. This means that one stage of development flows out of the previous stage, that a higher formation develops from a lower formation through a process of resolution of contradictry situations.

Historical Materialism

In Hegel's philosophy it was the "idea" that determined the course of natural and human events; "thought" thus became in his view the creator of outward realities and of the changes of these. This concept of historical development was brought to earth by Marx and Engels who, while adopting Hegel's general concept and method, postulated as the basic motive force of history not the "idea", the "thought", but material reality.

Marx, by adopting Hegel's dialectical method but rejecting his idealistic foundation, formulated the theory of "historical materialism" — that historical development is not the reflection of a self-developing spirit, but the expression of man's economic needs and wants.

In accordance with the principle of interrelation of phenomena occurring in the universe, historical materialism holds that society is a structurally interrelated whole. Any aspect of that whole — laws, education, science, art — can be understood only if it is considered in its relation to the others. Historical materialism, while accepting the idea of the interrelation of social phenomena, holds that there is one factor which determines the general form of a historical culture and which explains historical changes. This factor it finds in the modes of economic production and exchange.

Says Engels: "... *all* past history was the history of class struggles; ... these warring classes of society are always the product of the modes of production and exchange, in a word, of the *economic* conditions of their time; ... therefore the economic structure of society always forms the real basis from which, in the last analysis, is to be explained the whole superstructure of legal and political institutions, as well as of the religious, philosophical, and other conceptions of each historical period."[4] It is on the basis of the concept of economic determinism or economic necessity that Marx explains the historical changes from lower to higher forms of society.

According to historical materialism, changing methods of production come into conflict with existing property relations. These property relations become a fetter which by economic necessity are removed sooner or later. "In the development of the means of production of material goods needed for the existence of man, historical materialism sees the principal force which determines the whole social life of men, and conditions the passage from one social structure to another. The replacement of social-economic formations in history — primitive structure, communal organization, slaveholding society, the feudal, capitalist and socialist regimes — is before everything else the replacement of one set of production relations by another more progressive one. This replacement is always the cause and at the same time the necessary consequence of the development of productive forces in society."[5]

Historical Development Through the Clash of Contradictions

A transformation of the social-economic structure, according to the theory of historical materialism, operates through the dialectical process; and its essence is the resolution of contradictions at given historical stages. For example, within the womb of the feudal system there began to develop urban production; first, domestic manufacturing and later the large-scale industrial type. But the full development of these new forces was hampered by the persistence of feudal institutions, attuned to a society based on status relation between men. This status relation hindered the development of industrialism, which require freedom of contract. There arose a contradiction between feudalism and industrialism. In France, this contradiction was resolved through the Revolution of 1789, which brought to political power a new class, the bourgeoisie, the standard bearer of the newly developing industrialism. The victory of this class brought about a rearrangement in the basic aspect of social relations. The former "status" relation was replaced by the "contract" relation. Of the individual rights obtained through the Great French Revolution, freedom of contract was basic to the development of the new productive forces. The newly won political rights and the right of free contract became synthesized in a representative system of government. The contradictions between feudalism and industrialism were thus resolved through a change in the legislative, administrative and judicial systems brought about by the victorious struggle against the feudal privileged classes by the bourgeoisie with the aid of all those groups — the peasants, workers and artisans — who were also victims of feudalism.

As another example, applying to the stage of capitalism the thesis of dialectical development through the resolution of contradictions, the Marxian theory considers that within the present structure there has developed a contradiction between the mode of production and the appropriation of the fruits of production. Goods are produced by the collective work of thousands of workers centered around the huge modern industrial plants. But these goods, the product of collective effort, are appropriated to a large extent by the individual owners of the plant.

This leads to a situation under which those who produce do not get in wages their full share of the total production. The difference between this full share and their actual compensation is designated as "surplus-value", and is appropriated by the owners of the means of production. It is the private appropriation of the surplus-value which constitutes in the Marxian view the social impediment to fulfilling the purpose of the struggle with nature. That purpose, as the Marxians see it, is to provide the means of subsistence, for society as a whole, commensurate with the possibilities afforded by the highly developed technological devices. The proletariat and the other lower economic groups with highly restricted incomes are not able to purchase back the total amount of goods which they have produced. This deprives the lower economic groups of the full fruits of our highly perfected means of carrying forward the struggle with nature. The periodic accumulations of unsalable goods, in consequence of the private accumulation of surplus-value, lead to economic crises spelling distress for the workers. Since in the Marxian view the prime considerations under capitalism are profits and domination of markets rather than production these crises are interrelated with what Marxism calls "anarchy of production" resulting from a lack of planning. Under this system production is stepped up or slowed down in conformity with the view of individual capitalists as to their opportunities for profits and dominations of the markets. This motive force which was already observed by Marx and even before him by Saint-Simon and Robert Owen became of a determining significance with the advent of monopoly capitalism towards the turn of the century.

The economic crises resulting from these two factors — private appropriation of the surplus-value and unorganized production — were going, according to Marx, to increase in frequency and intensity, leading eventually to a social revolution. It is to be carried through by the industrial proletariat, who, because of its superior organization, will lead the agricultural workers. This revolution will bring about the socialization of the means of production and distribution and will thus resolve the contradictions inherent in capitalism.

Thus Marxism finds the means of an effective control of the social environment in the collectivization of the means of production and in the assumption of the political power by the working masses. In the Marxian view, property relations under collectivism will not allow the limitation of production for the benefit of the capitalists. The state will be under the direction of the actual producers, whose primary concern is not profits but full production, leading to the most widespread enjoyment possible of the fruits of the physical struggle with nature.

The Development of a Revolutionary Psychology

According to Marx, the transformation of lower types of social structure into higher ones through the resolution of social contradictions is a "jump-like" revolutionary process; and not a gradual, evolutionary one. It is the last stage of the process, formulated by Hegel, of transformation of quantity into quality, of a quantitative into a qualitative condition. To illustrate: in the course of the development of large-scale production, the small individual producers and the middle-class generally disappear, according to Marx. They turn into proletarians who increase in numbers and this increase in numbers leads to a new quality. "The cooperation of a number of people, the fusion of many forces into one single force, to use Marx's phrase, creates a 'new power' which is essentially different from the sum of its individual powers." [6] Applying this concept to the process of capital formation Marx, on the basis of the previous examination of constant and variable capital and surplus value draws the conclusion that "not every sum of money, or of value, is at pleasure transformable into capital. To effect this transformation, in fact, a certain minimum of money or exchange-value must be presupposed in the hands of the individual possessor of money or commodities."[7] Similarly, the increase in the numbers of proletarians produces a new quality, a "new power", the power of a revolutionary psychology which through disciplined organization will lead to a social revolution.

It is within this transformation of quantity into quality and in the consequent development of a revolutionary psychology, that the human element operates. It will either hasten or retard this development, depending upon the strength of the economic force as compared with that of the psychical and cultural forces which play upon the human being in a particular social aggregate. If the economic force is of such intensity as to weaken or eliminate the distinctive psychical and cultural characteristics of a given nationality, then this force will become predominant and lead to a revolutionary explosion.

The problem before us, if we want to avoid this danger is to obtain a comprehensive understanding of the operation in this country of the disruptive forces which — while they are violently opposed to Marxism — are unconsciously hastening the fulfillment of Marx's forecasts by their disregard of the American concept of economic freedom, the foundation of our economic system.

Especially in these days of uncertainty and world turmoil emotional patriotism must give way to a more far-seeing patriotism, based on the ability to detect certain enemies within our national economy. In the form of monopolies and cartels, they are the carriers of the Marxian idea and are a more threatening danger to our traditional economic and social ideals than any theories or states which are at variance with our historical ideals and traditions.

[1] Engels, Fredrich, *Anti-Duehring*, International Publishers, p. 30.

[2] Joyce O. Hertzler, *History of Utopian Thought*, 1923, pp. 310-311.

[3] G. W. F. Hegel, *Lectures on the Philosophy of History*. Bell and Daldy Yorkstreet, London, 1872, p. 51; and Fredrich Engels, *Anti-Duehring*, International Publishers, p. 31.

[4] Fredrich Engels, *Anti-Duehring*, International Publishers, p. 33.

[5] M. Rozental and P. Idin, editors, *Kratkii Filosofskii Slovar* (Short Philosophical Dictionary), Moscow, 1939, pp. 96-97.

[6] *Herr Eugene Duehring's Revolution in Science*, International Publishers, p. 144.

[7] *Ibid.*, p. 142.

CHAPTER V

Marxism and the Western World

Changes in the character and intensity of socio-historical forces are slow to penetrate into the consciousness of the people. The intensified action of certain economic forces which began to gather momentum with the passing of the frontier and which culminated in the depression of the thirties did, however, generate in the American people a hazy feeling that some basic change had occurred in the manner in which our economy functions.

In the early stages of the depression we were not overly worried. We were used to business cycles with their temporary and superficial economic dislocations. Even some of our outstanding economists and statisticians did not notice for a long while that this one was more than an ordinary depression — that it was in fact an economic crisis. The development of the crisis was stopped, before it came to full fruition, by the Herculean efforts of the Roosevelt administration; but it left a lasting impression upon the subconsciousness of the American people. It made us vaguely realize that we are not as much masters of our destiny as our achievements in overcoming natural obstacles in the conquest of the frontier had led us to believe. In fact, the almost overnight appearance of over ten million unemployed, the debacle of our agriculture with its tumbling prices and forced sales of mortgaged farms, and the staggering number of small business bankruptcies made us realize, in a general way, that our well-being was now meeting obstacles of a nature fundamentally different from those of the physical frontier.

The extent and intensity of the mass suffering which followed in the wake of the business collapse was without precedent in the history of the country. It gave us an uneasy feeling that some of the New Deal measures of the Roosevelt administration were at best palliatives. The very fact that the crisis had to be alleviated by such anti-social measures as a planned lowering of production and financial rewards for abstention from producing above a certain maximum, gave an impression of expediency.

We were skeptical as to the real value of these emergency acts. At the same time we generally overlooked the fact that, besides injecting into our economy certain unsound economic measures, which were

44

justified by the peculiarities of our price system and had to be resorted to in order to save the country from complete collapse, the Roosevelt administration was also engaged in activities directed toward a basic solution of our economic difficulties. Among other things it undertook to revive the enforcement of the Sherman Antitrust Act, a uniquely American approach to the problem presented by the economic contradiction of "poverty in the midst of plenty" which had lain practically dormant since its enactment in 1890.

Both antitrust legislation and Marxism are fundamentally concerned with the same problem — concentration of economic power as a deterrent to access to economic resources. Antitrust legislation, however, contemplates acting within the framework of our present social structure. On the other hand, Marxism believes that the ultimate solution of this problem lies in a complete reorganization of society on the basis of collectivization of the means of production and distribution.

Marxism is the first great revolutionary movement that challenges the age-old foundations of the institution of private property in the means of production. It presents a serious problem to capitalist countries and is the object of hatred and screeching propaganda. But a revolutionary movement, if it has its roots in the ground, cannot be stopped by a combination of fury, indignation, fear, and hysterical propaganda or by physical force. That Marxism is a real threat to a social order founded on the concept of freedom of opportunity cannot be denied. It has developed considerable strength at a time when the world was, and still is, disorganized following the two most destructive wars in history. When most of mankind find themselves in the throes of hunger, misery, and suffering they provide a fertile soil for the spread of a movement whose professed aim is to break with the old social order. For in the minds of many that order in the "old world" is associated with economic injustice, colonial exploitation and imperialistic oppression.

The anxiety exhibited in the statements of our public men and church leaders shows that we, in this country, feel that Marxism is a threat to our social order also; and this feeling is connected with a fear of the consequences of another possible crisis — that is, another depression. The first step in combating such a movement is through a proper understanding of its theoretical premises. A second is to make a careful analysis of conditions which would, on the one hand, foster, or, on the other, prevent the development of a revolutionary state of mind — in the Marxian view an inescapable consequence of the concentration of economic power in an industrialized society.

Marxism and the Western Proletariat

The questions at issue are these. Are the American people susceptible to a state of mind indicative of a possible social revolution in which the institution of private property in the means of production would be eliminated? Or, can our economic contradictions still be resolved within the framework of our social order through the democratic processes of legislation? In approaching the analysis of these phases of the problem which Marxism presents to a democratic society, we must turn from the consideration of objective economic forces to the study of subjective psychical characteristics. We must also consider these in the light of a general analysis of the interaction between objective and subjective forces.

According to Marxism, the breeding ground of a revolution lies in the psychical reactions of industrial workers. Deprived of the means of production and gathered in huge numbers in one place, these workers theoretically are susceptible to the development of a revolutionary spirit and are inclined to adopt organized militant action to a much greater extent than even the most oppressed agricultural population. And yet the first social revolution occurred not in the highly industrialized countries of America, England, Germany or France, but in Russia, which in 1917 was predominantly an agricultural country. As Maurice Dobb points out, "Most powerful of the currents that were carrying events toward the Soviet Revolution of November was the elemental movement among the peasants, who were effecting the seizure of the landed estates by direct action on a growing scale." [1] Unlike the previous elemental uprisings in the history of Russia this movement was consummated in a revolution owing chiefly to the leadership of the industrial workers in the large cities, principally in Petrograd (Leningrad).

Although Russian industry had been developing rapidly for several decades prior to the revolution, Russia was primarily a nation of a feudal-absolutist type; with a background totally different from the one which historical materialism or Marxism considers as a condition *sine qua non* of a revolutionary social reform. The Russian revolution, which took place under Marxist slogans and which established an economic order on Marxian principles, was the culmination of forces which were operating at that particular historical moment in Russia and which had no connection with the trend envisaged in the Marxian formula of transformation of quantity into quality.

On the other hand, America, with its tremendous industrial development and centralization, and probably the largest class of industrial workers in the world, has escaped a Marxian revolution. The transformation of quality into quantity and quantity into quality in this country has led, indeed, to an increase in the number of workers and to the development of their organizational capacity. But the organizations which have emerged as a result of this process are not animated by a revolutionary psychology; instead they display a pragmatic, trade-union state of mind.

This was also true of other capitalistic countries in the epoch before the first World War. In capitalistic countries, the population of which has, in one form or another, gone through the transition from quantity to quality, the transition did not have the effect of inculcating in the working class the desire to "guide and direct society toward revolution and communism." What has really occurred is a growth of trade-unionism, the philosophy of which is opposed to both communism and socialism.

The fact is that the democratic political form of government in the capitalist countries has been conducive to a state of mind which opposed the development of a revolutionary energy, the essential prerequisite of a social revolution. It was where democratic liberties did not exist, as in the pre-World War I Russia, that, despite the predominantly agricultural character of the population, the social revolution took place.

Marxism and the Middle-Class

A second postulate in the Marxian thinking is that centralization and concentration of industry must lead to the disappearance of the middle-class and the formation of a revolutionary state of mind among the industrial proletariat. So far as America and the Western European countries are concerned, political democracy has upset the working out of this formula. The middle-class in this country was preserved and, moreover, the trade-union movement has developed a middle-class outlook on life in the industrial worker, particularly in America.

Political democracy as evolved under capitalism in its role of a deterrent to the formation of a revolutionary proletarian state of mind is brought out by the late M. N. Pokrovski, an outstanding Soviet historian of the early days of the Soviet state. Speaking of the Russian worker, Pokrovski says:

"His origin from the most oppressed and hunted part of the peasantry, his factory environment which for his western comrades was a thing of the past, disclosed before him in sharp forms the desperate situation of the working and peasant classes in the conditions of the dictatorship of landed proprietors. Until the revolution there were absent the most necessary and elementary democratic liberties without which the proletariat could not conduct an effective struggle with capitalism. A strike was a criminal act. The trade-union and a workers' party was a political crime for participation in which the working-man paid with jail and exile. There was no parliament, and the access to such bodies as municipal and agrarian councils was barred to the workingman because of absence of property qualifications. If to the absence of political rights is added economic oppression and the continually decreasing standard of living of the proletarian classes then will be understood that historical fact which is presented by the most consistent and most decisive revolutionary psychology of the proletariat in Czarist Russia." [2]

The absence in Russia of economic and political rights led to the development of a revolutionary psychology which exploded in the communist revolution of October 1917. Although Pokrovski refers to the revolution of 1905, the conditions which followed this social outbreak continued despite the paper reforms which the Czarist government was compelled to grant the people in the fall of 1905 and which were largely nullified.

The development of political democracy in capitalist countries has fostered not a revolutionary but a middle-class mind. Social legislation engineered by Bismarck in Germany, the privileges granted labor in England by the Reform Bill consequent upon the Chartist movement, the development of trade-unions in France, Germany, England, Italy, and other countries have tended to evolve even in the socialist movements in Europe that pragmatic middle-class frame of mind which has not fulfilled the forecast of Marxism. The fact is that in the highly industrialized countries, this frame of mind prevented the development of the revolutionary ideology which, according to the Marxian theory, is a necessary prerequisite to a proletarian revolution.

The post-war developments in the Western European countries also bear strong testimony to the persistence of middle-class psychology as developed through the trade-union movement. After years of Hitler's absolutism and tyranny, in the midst of an acute economic crisis which followed the war and anxiety for the future the temper of the Western European proletariat is generally not revolutionary. In the continental Western European countries the communists, although they are showing considerable strength, are in a minority; the socialists, who represent a diluted form of Marxism and are basing their program not on revolution but on evolution are occupying a position of influence; there are, however, strong parties representing conservative tendencies and who have a considerable constituency of workers. As to England, the lack of revolutionary psychology is shown by the evolutionary program and the temper of the British Labor Party.

It is true that if we proceed further with our analysis we will find that the middle-class frame of mind in this country, which is more pronounced among our workers than in those of continental Europe, has economic premises; that it was formed, to a large extent, as a result of the homestead conquest of the frontier and the individualistic method of land settlement. But, we will also find that it was inherent in the psychical make-up of the English section of our population, which had a determining influence on our government and our economics and, in general, on the "tone" of our historical development. We will find, also, that it has acquired such strength and intensity as to exercise a determining influence on our industrial proletariat which, in the Marxian view, should be the breeding ground for the development of a revolutionary psychology.

The form of government in which is found the representative parliamentary system has produced the middle-class frame of mind even among non-middle-class members. In the case of America, it is further strengthened by the lingering influence of the frontier. This frame of mind asserts itself despite a growing inequality in the distribution of wealth and a high degree of centralization of production—that is, despite the concentration of economic power. The thoughts of our farmers run in the direction of obtaining cost of production, in the same way as a merchant's or manufacturer's mind is bent on obtaining an income that will cover his expenses. Our organized labor is as much middle-class as our farmers and businessmen. It has never demanded the nationalization of the means of production and it has never fought under slogans involving a complete reorganization of our national economy and government. Its avowed aim deals with the "American standard of living." At most, the farmers and workers put forward demands for a greater share in the national income. Even our protests and periodic revolts against Wall Street and monopolies are not carried on under the slogan of a complete reorganization of property relations. They lean, instead, toward a greater measure of control of financial, industrial, and business corporations.

To withstand the onslaught of forces which are turning the minds of the peoples in many countries of the world towards communism or socialism the people of America are in a favored position. Because of a combination of geographical location, and unexcelled industrial productivity, the peculiarities of the governmental organization, and especially the virility of their cultural inheritance they are in a more favored position than many other nations to control their social environment for the welfare of the country as a whole.

Cultural Factors and Marxian Difficulties in the Soviet Union

The significance and the strength of psychical and cultural factors is evident not only in America and in Western Europe but in Russia as well. It explains to a large extent the policies of the Soviet Union since the revolution which are accepted in certain quarters as deviations from, or even the abandonment of Marxism by the Soviet Government. These deviations should rather be considered as attempts to make Marxian economics workable by controlling the psychical factors, particularly the element of individualism, which were inherited from the previous social organization and which interefere with the progress of socialized economy.

The success of the application of the Marxian theory depends upon the presence of a collective psychology. A collective undertaking such as the nationalization of the country's economy on the principles of collectivism which contemplates the reorganization of the "way of life" of a nation cannot be carried out successfully in an environment in which individualistic tendencies have not disappeared.

The realization on the part of the Soviet Government of the strength of these tendencies showed itself in a number of ways during the first two decades after the Revolution as, for instance, in measures borrowed from the capitalist society. Among these should be mentioned the differentials in pay for work in factories and the granting of rewards to stimulate an increase in productivity. These measures were obviously designed to utilize for immediate purposes the individualistic motive force of self interest.

That a collective psychology was absent in Russia at the time of its social revolution is attested by the necessity in which the government found itself to enact the New Economic Policy (NEP) which reestablished free trade for a time but particularly by the fact that it had to resort to force to make its policy effective with regard to the collectivization of agriculture. And even then it had to allow the members of the collective the exclusive use of individual plots of land and permission to sell part of the products raised on the open market.

During the two decades preceding the second World War the aims of the Soviet Government appear to have been centered on developing in the people what the Russians call "obschestvennost" which means the sense of, and the desire for, participation in a collective enterprise. Aside from raising the productivity of agriculture, the establishment of collectives was aimed at developing a collective psychology in the peasantry. As in the case of agriculture the economic measures of the Soviet Government, supplemented by repression, were to be explained, to a large extent, in terms of policy designed to eliminate individualistic tendencies which, if not checked, would seriously threaten the success of the five-year plans and the ultimate realization of Russian collectivism.

Specifiic instances of the governmental policies which were formerly designed to foster the spirit of collectivism as well as to increase productive efficiency are the Machine Tractor stations the purpose of which is to supply mechanical power and machinery to the Kolkhozy (collective farms) A Soviet Machine Tractor Station, however, was not just a farm machinery custom work agency. It was also a "powerful arm of Soviet technical assistance, management, and control of collective agriculture, as well as a highly important fiscal instrument." [8] "In 1940, of a total of 523,000 tractors on farms, 435,300 belonged to the Machine Tractor Stations." [4]

The Soviet Government "which in the late 1920's was bent increasingly on collectivization of Russian agriculture, was quick to see that the Machine Tractor Stations would be a powerful lever for accomplishing (this) objective," [5] i.e., the collectivization of agriculture. But in addition to providing a concrete illustration of the possibilities of collectivized agriculture, the Machine Tractor Stations, through the office of an assistant or vice-director, were engaged in what can be called ideological activities. The function of this official was to develop in the farmers the consciousness of the need for collective effort to insure the success of a plan based on the collective principle of production.

It should be noted that the preceding discussion refers to the status of the Machine Tractor Stations as of the year 1940. Recent literature reveals the increasingly more drastic measures which the Soviet Government is adopting and which testify to the strength of the individualistic tendencies which have to be overcome to develop a spirit of collectivism in the Soviet Union which is a condition *sine qua non* of the success of a Socialist state. A considerable part of its cultural activities, even its fictional literature, is used as a medium of propaganda to impress upon the people the superiority of a collective over an individualistic economy. An instance of this propaganda in the domain of pedagogy is found in the following excerpt from an article in the *Sovietskaya Pedagogica* (Soviet Pedagogy) by a Soviet educator, A. S. Makarenko. Speaking of parental authority, he says:

"The chief basis of parental authority can only be a better life and work of the parents, their civic entity, their conduct . . . The civic authority of the parents will attain its highest level when this authority is (that) of a member of a group. If you succeed in bringing up your son so that he will be proud of the entire factory where his father works . . . then you have reared him correctly . . . Our life is the life of socialist society. Father and mother must appear before their children as participants in this life." [6]

It is difficult to foresee what the future holds with respect to the possibility of a maturing of collectivism in the Soviet Union. It is more than probable that the present ultra-dictatorial form of government will sooner or later give way to a more democratic political system. In view, however, of the absence of the free enterprise tradition in that country, the already established socialization of the means of production and distribution may in the long run lead to its complete acceptance by the people of the Soviet Union. It may then present us with a real threat. Our ability to meet it will depend upon giving free field to the expression of enlightened individualism which is stifled by the economic imbalances of our social organization. This is of particular significance to us both from domestic and international considerations.

In view of the advance of communism in many important areas of the world, our domestic and international problems are welded into one. As Michael Straight expresses it in an article in the *New Republic*: "Their [the Russians'] program is to achieve world conquest by exploiting the inner weaknesses of democracy. To the extent that we concentrate on the cold war and ignore the developing imbalances within our society, we play into Soviet hands." [7]

Apart from the question of the cold war or the threat of a real war there is grave danger to our social system in the disparity between the growing collectivism of monopoly capitalism and the enlightened individualism which is the quintessence of the distinctive American way-of-life. We are faced with the problem of bringing the objective conditions of our existence into harmony with the subjective motive forces which have moulded our outlook on life.

We can attain this goal if we bring into full play the cultural inheritance known as the American tradition which forms the distinctive characteristic of our aims and aspirations. If given a proper stimulus to legislation which aims at eliminating social and economic imbalances this precious inheritance will enable us to withstand the onslaught of alien forces on our society. We must choose between capitalism and socialism. If we want to make capitalism work we must weaken monopoly in every field of economic endeavor. This applies also to such proposals as those of a "mixed economy," and other palliatives which will prove sterile in a monopolistic environment.

[1] Maurice Dobb, *Soviet Economic Development Since 1917*, International Publishers, pp. 74-75.

[2] M. N. Pokrovski, "The Revolution of 1905," *The Bolshevik*, October, 1934.

[3] "Machine Tractor Stations," *Foreign Agriculture*, U. S. Department of Agriculture, April 1948, p. 80.

[4] *Ibid.*, p. 80.

[5] *Ibid.*, p. 80.

[6] Quoted from "Russia's New Morality," Jerry Talmer, *Nation*, November 26, 1949.

[7] Michael Straight, "The Right Way to Beat Communism," *New Republic*, May 1, 1950.

CHAPTER VI

Social Control and the American Tradition

In the age-old problem of attempting to control social environment the American tradition plays a unique role, inasmuch as it is preoccupied with the search for the ideal of a social welfare interwoven with political rights and the economic freedom of the individual.

America is unlike the countries in which a history full of oppression has led fatalistically to violent attempts at the solution of social problems. In contrast, the history of America presents a remarkable blend of social and economic factors which point toward peaceful evolutionary progress, through a conscious social control free from subservience to blind historical forces. The peculiar motive forces which determine the character of the American tradition are associated with the pragmatic outlook on life—the resultant of the blend of Anglo-Saxon inheritance with the spirit of the frontier—colored by Jeffersonian idealism. This fusion of inheritance and environment has led to a distinctive relation between the antagonistic social forces of action and counteraction; one of which represents the oppressive force, the other, the protesting force.

The theory of Marxism implies that the oppressive force, i.e., capitalist exploitation through ownership of the means of production, inevitably generates a protesting force of revolutionary nature among the industrial proletariat. But the developments in the Western democracies, particularly in America, have upset this prognosis. The juridical and political consequences of the unfolding of capitalism there, have led to a different mode of counteraction than that envisaged by Marx. An expanding capitalism should presuppose freedom of contract, opportunities for accomplishment regardless of birth and social status, and, in general, freedom in social and political intercourse. Following the economic disorganization occasioned by the industrial revolution, the fighting spirit of the Western European proletariat was, it is true, rising high in pursuance of these ends. But the fact that the social and political relations in capitalism there were interwoven with a representative system of government contributed immeasurably to the weakening of this revolutionary temper.

The parliamentary method circumscribed the rule of the government and of the governing classes. This provided a safety valve for popular discontent. Instead of leading to revolutionary upheavals, the struggle of the industrial workers for economic justice was channeled into trade-union activities; and was directed principally toward a gradual improvement of the working and living conditions of the laboring masses. Another important factor in developing among the industrial workers an evolutionary attitude toward social problems was connected with the relative prosperity consequent upon the expansion of capitalism and its exploitation of colonies for the benefit of the mother countries.

In the case of Russia, the relation between action and counteraction was of a fundamentally different character. The full expansion of capitalism was obstructed by the survival of the absolutist-feudal system. The autocratic government refused to tone down appreciably the violence of its repressive policies, even after the Revolution of 1905 which established a parody of a parliamentary system. Continuing violent action on the part of the government and the ruling classes provoked an equally violent counteraction which led to the revolutionary explosion of 1905, and later to the Revolution, first of March and then of October, 1917.

Action and Counteraction in Western Europe in the 19th Century

The specific manifestations of the relation between action and counteraction vary in individual nations. The variations depend upon a conglomeration of factors which in their totality determine the outlook on life of a given national entity. In this respect there is a difference not only between capitalist democracies and the more or less feudal agricultural countries, but between capitalist nations themselves, notably between Western Europe and America. It is this difference, itself, that opens up a range of possibilities for meeting our own problems in an evolutionary instead of a revolutionary way, despite the fact that America has evolved toward a nation-wide interdependent industrial economy which is eliminating a significant motive of our past history — sectionalism. That is, the history of Western Europe since the Great French Revolution of 1789, expressed in terms of fluctuations between action and counteraction, is of particular significance and assistance to us as we try to crystallize our problem in meeting the threat of expanding influence of Marxian theories.

Western Europe presents in a compact form, within a period of a little over a century, a picture of social movements of a political and economic nature which gave rise to revolutionary theories. The seeds of these social movements are to be found in the period of transition between the industrial revolution and the fruition and expansion of capitalism in the latter half of the 20th century. That is, the economic dislocations in Western European countries which followed the industrial revolution, and which were particularly marked during the first half of the nineteenth century, led to social movements of a revolutionary type. The influence of the revolutionary theories in various countries fluctuated with the fluctuating relations between action and counteraction.

In England, there was the Chartist movement in the thirties of the past century, which represented a revolt of the working classes against intolerable working conditions and curtailment of political rights. It led in the long run to the enactment of legislation known as the Reform Bill, extending parliamentary representation to the hitherto disfranchised elements of the British population. The action of the British government and ruling classes in thus using the key institution of democracy, the Parliament, in submitting to the demands of the workers, channeled organized discontent away from revolution into the trade-union movement, which has an evolutionary philosophy. In accordance with law, the trade-unions have since continued to battle for better working and living conditions through a combination of economic and political action.

The social movements in France and in other Western European countries present, *mutatis mutandi*, a similar picture. France, as a result of economic dislocations and the instability of democratic institutions in the period before 1870, went through the revolution of 1830 and 1848, and revolutionary upheavals such as the Lyons insurrection in 1831 and in 1870 the Paris Commune. After the Commune was crushed, France entered the era of political democracy which was to last until June 1940, when the country collapsed under the onslaught of the Nazis. In other parts of Europe, notably in Austria, Hungary and Germany, revolutions took place in 1848. But the extension of the parliamentary system in these countries, combined with the expansion of capitalism and the social and economic reforms of the Bismarckian period in Germany, came to afford a certain measure of economic security. Violent counteractions — revolutions and revolutionary upheavals — passed into a milder form of counteraction; based, as in England, on a combination of economic and political struggles for improvement of the conditions of the workers. We must remember that the revolutionary upheavals of which we have been speaking took place in the period before the fruition of capitalism. However, with the development and expansion of capitalism, with the development of colonies and the strengthening of the representative system of government, the revolutionary temper of the masses of Western Europe practically disappeared. During the rest of the century and up to the eve of the first world war the activities of the workers were directed toward improving, by means of organization and intermittent economic strikes, the conditions of labor, such as wages, hours, social security, unemployment benefits and consumers' cooperatives. Socialist organizations continued to exist and even to grow, particularly the Social Democratic Party. But their program maximum, a socialist society, was left to a large extent in the realm of a pious wish. Socialists concentrated their strength on the program minimum, involving the improvement of the economic and political status of labor within the framework of the capitalist society.

In his *General Strike*, Jean Jaurès, the famous French Socialist, says: "Socialism has only one high level tactics — a *peaceful* conquest of power through parliamentarism."

Gustave Hervé, a French Socialist leader of the pre-World War I days, states: "In the whole of Western Europe the socialist parties under their revolutionary appearance are holding to a line which hardly can be conceived by the Russian socialists who have not yet tasted the delights of parliamentarism and of the electoral excitement. With the exception of Russia, everywhere the socialist parties have been transformed into parties of *legal reforms*." [1]

The idea of an international revolution remained as a nebulous concept to be revived in oratory at international congresses and May Day demonstrations. Its comparative lack of support among the masses, as time went on, is evidenced by the readiness with which the Western European Socialist parties—notably the strongest of them, the German Social Democratic Party—flocked to their national colors at the outbreak of the war in 1914.

Basis of Difference Between Revolutionary and Evolutionary Theory

The upheavals which preceded the fruition of capitalism saw the birth of certain theories based upon the deterministic concept of the role of property in social relationships. Looking toward a revolutionary reorganization of society, these theories aimed at a fundamental reorganization of the economic system through the elimination of private property — either by nationalizing the instruments of production, as in Marxism, or by establishing cooperative production enterprises, as in the case of the anarchists and the utopian socialists. The anarchist Proudhon's slogan "Property is Theft" — was a blunt expression of the point of view of leaders of the revolutionary mass movements and of their followers. In other words, their concept was that all social and economic evils have their source in the institution of private property and that the role of the state is to enforce by violence perpetuation of this institution.

The statement of revolutionary theory in the "Communist Manifesto" of Marx and Engels, published in 1848, had a considerable influence on the proletarian masses of Europe. Its thesis revolves around property as the crucial problem of history and stresses the role of the revolutionary class struggle in the reorganization of society on new and fundamentally different property relationships. Its philosophical foundadation is that of materialistic monism, the doctrine which refers all phenomena to, or derives them from, a single ultimate material constituent or agent. Marxism is materialistic monism in that it attributes all the negative phenomena of social life to the economic factor — to the institution of private property in the means of production and distribution. It considers that this institution leads to class differentiation and class struggles, and that class struggles have determined the course of history in its economic as well as its cultural manifestations. The direct corollary of this concept, of course, is that the solution of the economic contradictions presented by capitalism is the socialization of the means of production and distribution which involves a complete reorganization of society.

The evolutionary pragmatic state of mind of today, on the other hand, while it may also consider certain causes as fundamental and others as auxiliary, is pluralistic. It rejects the application of a general theory, based on a single deterministic principle to the solution of social contradictions; it thinks in terms of concrete relations presented by a particular problem. Instead of a complete reorganization of society it aims at proceeding gradually through the transformation of lower forms of social relationships into higher ones. As an instance, a trade-union fights for collective bargaining not on the basis of an abstract theory of surplus-value but on the idea of replacing a lower form of relationship — that between unorganized workers and employers who can impose their will upon their employees — with a higher form of relationship under which organized workers have acquired a certain degree of strength which enables them to oppose arbitrary treatment. The latter is a higher form of relationship because it is better balanced and hence leads to greater justice in the relations between the two parties. It is this concept of improvement in social relationships that counteracted in Western Europe the influence of Marxism when the representative system of government became solidly established and gave birth to liberal socialistic theories of the Fabian variety.

Pragmatism and American Thought

America did not have the kind of revolutionary upheavals which were shaking Europe before 1870. While the capitalist countries of Western

Europe went through oscillations between revolutionary and evolutionary attitudes, the people of America, in attempting to solve their social and economic problems, held steadily to the evolutionary point of view. This is also a direct consequence of the pragmatic outlook on life, conditioned largely by a distinctive economic environment, which is the essential characteristic of the American people.

The components of the American pragmatic outlook on life were formulated in that essentially American school of thought — pragmatism. The basic characteristic of pragmatism is that it is pluralistic; that it considers that social relationships are determined by a variety of causes, in contrast to the Marxian monistic materialism which views social relationships as determined by one factor — the struggle of classes conditioned by property relations. This fundamental difference between these two schools of thought leads to the difference in their views concerning the nature of the evolution of history. Marxism holds to the fatalistic view; it considers that the class struggle is a fatalistic force which drives humanity toward a social revolution and a socialist organization of society. Pragmatism, on the other hand, assigns an important role to the human will. It considers that social and economic problems are solved through gradual improvements in all spheres of human relations, while Marxism holds that these problems can be solved only through a reorganization of property relations. Pragmatism is essentially an individualistic philosophy adapted to a nation like America which developed a continent through the efforts of individual frontiersmens.

Early pragmatism centered its attention on particular relationships without attempting to unify these relationships through the operation of a single, all-pervading cause. It held that these relationships should be representative of particular experiences. The deductive process of reasoning was banished and the test of truth was the practical result. It was solely interested in actual detached experiences rather than in a unifying principle which, it considered, led to determinism. In this form it was essentially a philosophy adapted to the rugged individualism of the 19th century. In fact, it was conditioned by it.

American pragmatism, however, stands apart not only from the pluralistic schools of Western Europe but from that of the other Anglo-Saxon country, England, as well. The formation of the American pragmatic tradition is due to the spirit generated by the individualistic conquest of the frontier blended with the legacy of England through the contributions of Locke to American political theory, and to the empirical spirit of English thinking, which is the foundation of pragmatism.

The distinctive American origin of pragmatism is brought out in the following excerpt from *Growth of the American Republic* by Samuel E. Morison and Henry S. Commager:

"It was natural that pragmatism should have received its earliest statement and most elaborate formulation in the United States, for to a striking degree pragmatism accommodates itself to the American environment and suits the American temper. 'It is beyond doubt,' says John Dewey, 'that the progressive and unstable character of American life and civilization has facilitated the birth of a philosophy which regards the world as being in a constant formation where there is still place for indeterminism, for the new, for a real future'." [2]

Philosophical systems do not originate in a vacuum. They have their roots in the outlook on life of a given people as conditioned by social forces and national characteristics. In the case of the 19th century America, these forces had their origin in the frontier method of expansion of the American continent as well as in the "ideas and attitudes" which we inherited from England, whose national traits and whose concepts of law, government and political institutions form our historical foundation.

Pragmatism and the Frontier Spirit

In his discussion of the social foundations of the pragmatic outlook on life in America, Dr. Horace M. Kallen — an outstanding exponent of pragmatism and the closest co-worker of the late William James — points out that the frontier developed the habit of speculation in terms of concrete relationships rather than an abstract approach to the problems presented by the social environment.

"It was in the conditions of the American countryside," says Dr. Kallen, "that a pragmatic reaction took place against monistic determinism which in the early Puritan days of our history was represented by Calvinism, a deterministic doctrine which originated in the conditions of the Puritan revolution in England in the 17th century.

"The countryside was first and last wilderness and frontier. Those who dwelt in it or wandered over it were pioneers gambling with the uncertainties of climate, soil, animals and Indians, risking their lives and fortunes on an unknown future. For these actual risks the certainties of Calvinistic predestination could serve only as imaginative compensations. Pioneer life dissolved the inevitabilities of this tradition into the chances and changes of the struggle for existence in the wilderness. With them were worn down all the fixed orders or inherited caste and custom. Achievement replaced status as the measure of value. Rank and birth gave way to works. Men ceased to be born good, they 'made' good. That pregnant Americanism tells the story. It shows that considerations of the past have given way to creations of the future, that what is from day to day vital to Americans is not established order, routine and finality, but initiative, enterprise, innovation, and that these are judged not by their premises but by their consequences.

"Industry exhibits an analogous transformation of mood. Its captains risked not so much their lives as their fortunes. But its rank and file, who filled the textile factories, laid the railroads, dug the ores and smelted the metals, came first adventuring from the countryside, with the habit of initiative and experiment strong in them. Later they were partly pushed upward and largely supplemented by immigrants from all over Europe. Thus industrial enterprise in America elicited, from both native and immigrant whites, attitudes, qualities and valuations like those of the wilderness. The mood was continental."[3]

What should especially be noted is the reference to the fact that under frontier conditions "achievement replaced status as the measure of value" and that "rank and birth gave way to works." In Western Europe with the establishment of democratic institutions, achievement also replaced status as a measure of value both in law and in custom. However, the old feudal distinctions of class and caste not only lingered but continued to exercise considerable influence in social, and to a large extent in economic, relationships. In fact, in a number of countries which threw off feudalism in favor of capitalism, large landed estates continued to be concentrated in the hands of the nobility; notably in Germany, England, and Italy. In America the social distinctions have never had more than a negligible influence; but the fact of achievement was of genuine significance. The favorite boast of the "self-made" men, the captains of industry, of whom our upper economic groups were in the past largely composed, was that they came up from the economically lower strata of society. On the other hand, as a result of wide opportunities, the aspirations of the members of the lower economic groups gravitated towards the attainment of a status outside their group. It is this that Lenin had in mind when he once remarked that the possibilities of social revolution in America are dim, inasmuch as the capitalist has a workingman's psychology and the workingman has a capitalist's psychology.

A number of other factors contributed to the intense feeling of personal achievement — factors which were also connected with wider opportunities than in the Western European countries — such as free access to high schools and greater opportunities for university education through the possibility of that typical American phenomenon, "working one's way through college," which was almost unknown in Europe. Physical work, even of the lowest kind, was never looked upon here with derision as it was even in the European democracies despite the latter's juridical rejection of "status" in favor of "achievement."

From the point of view of the relation between action and counter-action the frontier had a lasting moderating influence on the social movements in this country throughout the entire period of the evolution of capitalism. It forestalled the development of a spirit of acute social discontent at a crucial period in the history of capitalist countries — in the days when the effects of the industrial revolution on the working classes kept Western Europe in a revolutionary fermentation for several decades. The meaning of the frontier as a social safety valve was brought out by the German philosopher G. W. F. Hegel (1770-1831) in his *Lectures on the Philosophy of History*, published in the 1820's. Says Hegel:

"America has the outlet of colonization constantly and widely open; and multitudes are continually streaming into the plains of the Mississippi. By this means the chief source of discontent is removed, and the continuation of the existing civil condition guaranteed. A comparison of the United States of North America with European lands is therefore impossible; for in Europe, such a natural outlet for population, notwithstanding all the emigrations that take place, does not exist. Had the woods of Germany been in existence, the French Revolution would not have occurred. North America will be comparable with Europe only after the immeasurable space which that country presents to its inhabitants shall have been occupied, and the members of the political body shall have begun to be pressed back on each other."[4]

Seventy years later this thought was given expression by Frederick Jackson Turner in his noted essay *The Significance of the Frontier in American History*.[*] Says this American historian: "Whenever social conditions tended to crystalize in the East, whenever capital tended to press upon labor or political restraints to impede the freedom of the mass, there was this gate of escape [the free land] to the free conditions of the frontier. . . . Men would not accept inferior wages and a permanent position of social subordination when this promised land of freedom and equality was theirs for the taking."[5]

Individualism Modified by Jeffersonian Idealism

The early New England Calvinism played a considerable part in developing the spirit of individualism. "They [the New Englanders] held that the relations between God and man were regulated by contract, and this idea of contract they transferred to the other relations of life. Thus they had long based their political systems upon the theory, afterwards formulated by Locke and expressed in the Declaration of Independence, that government must rest on the consent of the governed, preferably expressed in the form of a written contract or constitution." [6]

The blend of inherited and environmental factors developed the pragmatic outlook on life. This, however, was modified by a stream of an idealistic nature which went beyond the consideration of detached experiences. This stream which dates back to the origins of this republic, is expressed in vivid terms in the Preamble of the Declaration of Independence: "We hold these truths to be self-evident, that all men are created equal, that they are endowed by their creator with certain inalienable rights, that among these are Life, Liberty and the pursuit of Happiness."

This wording goes beyond the concept of detached relationships. It proclaims a general principle of an ethical nature. Coupled with the rest of the preamble and the body of the Declaration of Independence it makes of this great historical document a symbol of the American mind as it was formed in the environment of a virgin continent. It welds into a harmonious whole, expressed in "phrases of haunting beauty",[7] the variegated pattern of the motive forces of the development of the American nation. It is a consonant unity of the philosophy of natural rights, of the influence of the French encyclopaedists, of Locke's theory of social compact, of the English legacy of empiricism and of the individualistic spirit of the frontier. It represents in the last analysis the synthesis of utilitarianism and idealism which found expression in modern times in the works of John Dewey and which contributed to a concept of a higher order than the early crude pragmatism which is still all too common. The crude type of pragmatism does not connect detached experiences and specific relations; it shies away from generalizations from facts, and, as a consequence, it does not see the forest because of the trees in human relationships. It develops at best into an anaemic phenomenon-eclectism. It does not realize that generalization does not necessarily lead to determinism.

It is the ethical factor that Jefferson injected into the Preamble of the Declaration that made this document, the body of which is empirical, the symbol of the higher order of pragmatic thinking.

Vernon L. Parrington points out that, "in the major doctrines of his political philosophy Jefferson was an amalgam of English and French liberalisms, supplemented by the conscious influence of the American frontier. That fusion early took place in his mind." When in the years to come "he drafted the Declaration of Independence the fusion was complete." [8]

Parrington further states that, "the strong influence of French humanitarianism was revealed in the passage on slavery that was stricken out on the floor of Congress and more significantly in the change in the familiar phrasing of the several natural rights. Samuel Adams and other followers of Locke had been content with the classical enumeration of life, liberty, and property; but in Jefferson's hands the English doctrine was given a revolutionary shift. The substitution of 'pursuit of happiness' [in the Declaration of Independence] for 'property' marks a complete break with the Whiggish doctrine of property rights that Locke had bequeathed to the English middleclass, and the substitution of a broader sociological conception; and it was this substitution that gave to [the Declaration of Independence] the note of idealism which was to make its appeal so perennially human and vital." [9]

The substitution of the idea of "pursuit of happiness" for "property" reveals in Thomas Jefferson the consciousness of an ideal far beyond and above the defense of the violated rights for which the colonies fought. The fact that the preamble was not even called into question during the debate on the Declaration shows that the representatives of the colonies assembled in the Continental Congress at Philadelphia were conscious of the idealistic side of the conflict with Great Britain. This should be expected in a revolutionary struggle which, despite the fact that it was waged primarily for the re-conquest of specific rights, was animated by a lofty idealism as is attested by the influence of Thomas Paine, Samuel Adams and the other lesser ideological leaders of the Revolutionary War.

Jefferson's concept of social justice was fused in the preamble with Locke's theory of social compact which, as Padover points out, "was the dominant doctrine of the middle-class" [10] and "was the experience of Americans on this new continent." [11] This theory was expressed in the stirring words of which only the first seven are remembered by the average American: "When in the course of human events it becomes necessary for one people to dissolve the political bonds which have connected them with another . . . a decent respect for the opinions of mankind requires that they should declare the causes which impel them to the separation."

The general principles of the preamble are followed in the body of the Declaration by specific charges levelled against the British government in the person of George III. Jefferson's arraignment of this monarch is a masterful treatment of the great problems with which the revolting colonies were confronted. "With the cleverness of a subtle manipulator", says Padover, "he [Jefferson] personalized the enemy and exposed him to devastating attack. Instead of accusing the British nation, Jefferson singled out George the Third as the *diabolus ex machina*, and delivered him short, relentless jabs." [12]

The lasting value of the specific charges levelled at the then king of Great Britain lies in the fact that they are a concrete expression of the general principles of social justice enunciated in the preamble. These principles permeate the practical statements which form the body of the Declaration. "Jefferson summed up not only the reasons which impelled Americans to independence, but the political and social principles upon which the Revolution itself rested." [13] The philosophical outlook of Thomas Jefferson contributed a potent factor of an ethical nature to social relations. Morison and Commager state that, "America is still indebted to Jefferson's principles for whatever liberalism and idealism she has preserved in an industrial society." [14]

As William T. Evjue points out: "With the development of industrialization, the rise of great monopolistic corporations, and the consequent ever-spreading antisocial use of property, Jeffersonian idealism was translated into concrete terms dealing with the various phases of our economic life. Jefferson's idealistic concept of human rights found expression in numerous laws, State and Federal, which regulate economic relationships in the light of social justice and consideration for popular rights. These laws were manifestations of progressive thought which were flowing throughout the breadth of this land. To mention only a few, there was the administration of Andrew Jackson, the apostolic crusade of William Jennings Bryan, the antitrust activities of Woodrow Wilson as governor of New Jersey, the work of LaFollette in Wisconsin, and the social reforms of Franklin D. Roosevelt." [15]

The American Tradition and Monopolies

The strength of the components of the American tradition was conditioned to a large extent by the expansion of our territory and our national economy. The economic disturbances which occurred every now and then, such as the several business depressions, were indicative of certain maladjustments, but they did not have serious consequences. So long as there was free land in existence and as there appeared no visible limit to the possibilities of expansion, these periodical dislocations did not attract sustained attention. But these dislocations were the first feeble manifestations of a new force which was developing in our economy, a force which in the years to come was to gather momentum and to become a dominant problem of our economic life. This was the concentration of economic power.

The real significance of this problem lies in the possibility that, through the development of economic forces inimical to what is known as the American way of life, the psychology of the American people as it bears on the question of the solution of economic problems may undergo a change. The essence of our psychology as a nation has been enlightened empiricism. As such it militates against the consideration of a revolutionary monistic solution of social problems. It is evolutionary in that it envisages the peaceful transition from lower to higher forms of social relationships through the process of democratic legislation. The blend of inherited Anglo-Saxon traits with those developed through the frontier struggle and enlightened by Jeffersonian idealism lends a distinction of its own to the American outlook on life. Known as the American tradition, the essence of which is pragmatic thinking animated by ethical considerations, this outlook on life sets our nation apart not only from communistic countries but also from the Western European democracies.

The distinctiveness of the American tradition shows itself strikingly in the attitude of our working classes towards employers. The kind of class consciousness which animates the proletariat of the European industrial nations is seldom found in the United States. "Research has shown," says John W. McConnell, "that the American working man readily identifies himself as a member of the 'working class' but means by that a class which includes everyone who works for a living; and antagonism to the 'boss', where it exists is highly personalized and crops out only as mutuality of interest collapses occasionally before a specific point of conflict." [16] However, Dr. McConnell points out "that tendencies toward the sharpening of class differences in the United States are becoming increasingly apparent" [17] and that "election statistics show a progressive disintegration of regional loyalties in favor of groupings around the economic interests of functional groups." [18] To support his view Dr. McConnell cites what he designates as the "unbelievable popularity" of the Roosevelt-Truman social welfare legislation and the tremendous growth of labor organizations.

The unimpeded development of monopoly capitalism will undoubtedly work toward a greater sharpening of class differences with a negative effect on the American labor movement which so far has been characteristically pragmatic and devoid of a deterministic outlook on life.

Since the American tradition presents a fusion of several factors, cultural as well as environmental, the weakening of any one of these will tend to divert it in an un-American direction. It may make the American people more susceptible to the influence of radical, rather than evolutionary, thinking. As we have seen, the motivating force in the formation of the American pragmatic outlook on life was the moving frontier. This offered mass opportunities of access to economic resources which in those days were largely natural resources. The popular slogan which expressed the idea of such opportunities was "free enterprise," and free enterprise became the guiding star of all those who were loyal to the American tradition. As a medium of competitive opportunities of access to economic resources, free enterprise is interwoven with free competition. Any economic force, therefore, that invalidates free competition is destructive of the American tradition. It involves the danger of weakening our pragmatic attitude towards our social environment. It lessens our opportunities for a conscious democratic control of our social environment, and it may change the relation between action and counteraction in the direction of a more radical opposition to intensified economic oppression.

A force of such economic oppression is at work in the American economy under the form of concentrated private economic power. The significance of the part which it was to play in the national economy of the country first came to the attention of the American people in the form of farmer's movements—those of the Grange and the Farmers' Alliance (Populist Party). The agitation attendant upon these movements influenced the Congress of the United States to devote serious attention to the nascent development of concentrated economic power as it was manifested in monopolies and monopolistic practices. This led to the enactment in 1890 of the Sherman Antitrust Act, the avowed purpose of which is to stimulate free enterprise through the prosecution and elimination of monopolies. The historical significance of this Act lies in the fact that it was passed about the time the frontier was reached and the freedom of movement restricted, with the resultant contraction of opportunities of access to economic resources. It had become less and less possible to find a social safety valve in the new lands. It was evident that we were confronted with the problem of readjusting our economic relations within the new restricted area in which our economy was operating.

The advance towards the frontier had been followed by a continuous industrial and business expansion. But as the last frontier was being reached emphasis was shifting to business policies which reflected the gradual contraction of the area of economic activities. Expansion means freedom of competition and an increasing utilization of productive resources. The subordination of production policies to the exclusive consideration of profit security and market domination, coupled with the ever-growing restraints upon competition, indicated that econ-

omic expansion in its true sense had given way to contraction. As
Thorstein Veblen points out in his "Absentee Ownership," the old cap-
tain of industry who thought in terms of production had been replaced
by the type of business leader who, in subordinating production to
monopolistic and financial manipulations, had become the "absentee
owner" in American industry. Monopolistic market domination, rather
than the full utilization of economic resources, became the dominant
motive force in our national economy. As a consequence, a full utilization of the human resources was gravely impaired, with detrimental
effects upon the national economy. The enactment of the Sherman
Antitrust Act at the time of the passing of the frontier is significant,
in view of the fact that antitrust legislation seeks to reopen competitive
opportunities of access to economic resources through the elimination
of monopolistic practices.

The New Frontier in Relation to Historical Perspective

The conquest of the physical frontier was completed over a century
ago, but there emerged a new frontier — the frontier of intangible bar-
riers which obstruct the free play of the forces of competition. To help
the American people to achieve the conquest of this economic frontier
of anti-competitive policies is the mission of antitrust legislation. With
the emergence of this new frontier the problem of the control of environment took on a different aspect. The conquest of the physical
frontier involved the control of the physical environment; the conquest
of the economic frontier involves the control of the social environment.
This change in the relation of the American people to their environment necessitates a reappraisal of the general problem of man's mastery
over his environment as applied to American conditions.

The frontier with its obstacles and dangers was subdued through the
efforts of individuals. Within a comparatively short period of time
the individual frontiersman had built up from complete wilderness an
empire which is without equal today. This developed in the American
people the feeling that man's superiority over nature had its source
in the freedom of the will. The freedom of the will of the frontiersman
revealed itself in his fearlessness, in his disregard of dangers and hardships, in his persistence in attaining his goal despite failures and dis-
appointments and in expressions of his pragmatic thinking. This freedom of the will was to a large extent, however, illusory. The physical
environment was made subservient to man less through sheer willpower
than through control, in a crude form, of the law of causality in the
struggle with nature. It was a brilliant achievement of "subduing
nature by obeying her," [19] in the words of Sir Francis Bacon of Verulam.

The successful efforts in controlling the laws of causality with respect to the physical environment have had the effect of blinding us to the difficulties presented by the infinitely more complicated problem of controlling the laws of causality in the field of social relationships. The result is that, when we are confronted with an economic crisis such as that of the thirties, we take the attitude that, without regard to the forces which have shaped our historical development, we can rearrange our social relationships at will by devising blueprints of a supposedly more efficient working of the social mechanism.

An extreme variety of such blueprints devised some years ago was known as "Technocracy." It evoked considerable support and attention from laymen and from academic circles. Struck by the triumphant march of industrialization, the plan unfolded the picture of an ideal social order to be run by technological experts. In its essence, it was the 20th century version of Plato's utopia. Plato's theory of "Philosopher-Kings" who were to govern his utopia through justice — which in the Greek mind was associated with reason — was to be put into effect in the visions of the technocrats, through the substitution of "Engineer-Kings" for "Philosopher-Kings."

Other plans and blueprints which deal with the solution of our social and economic problems, although much less sanguine than technocracy, exhibit a similar lack of historical perspective. They overlook the fact that out past continues to live within ourselves, that it has molded our outlook on life, that it is part of ourselves, and that any thought of modification in our economic relationships must be in harmony with the forces which have determined our historical development.

Likewise, it is the lack of consonance between the past and the present that lies at the bottom of the obstacles which the building of a socialist society on communist lines presents in the Russia of today. It accounts for the difficulties with which the government of the U.S.S.R. is confronted in endeavoring to harmonize the psychology of the people with the communist social order which came into being abruptly after a centuries-old feudal-absolutist state.

The Acquisitive Instinct and Restraints on Antisocial Use of Property

The basic difficulty in the carrying out of socialism is the persistence of the acquisitive instinct. The strength of this factor is acknowledged by the Soviet government. On collective farms it allots a number of hectares of land to each member of the collective in full ownership, with the right to sell the products of such allotments on the open market. Premiums for exceptionally efficient work in industry, payments for piece work and other similar measures testify to the strength of the acquisitive instinct the elimination of which forms the substance of the efforts of the Soviet Union to develop a collective psychology as was brought out in an earlier chapter. The potency of this instinct is attested by the fact that it still persists despite the socialization of the means of production and distribution in the Soviet Union.

Marxism seeks to render impotent the acquisitive instinct by excluding it from that area of economic activities in which it is the most virulent in its effects upon social relationships, namely, in the realm of private ownership of the means of production and distribution. True to its monistic outlook, Marxism seeks to bring this about through the socialization of the means of production and distribution — a social arrangement which does not harmonize with the motive forces of American life and which can be brought about in a *true* sense only through a social revolution.

The essence of the problem of social control in a society based on freedom of competition is associated with the task of harmonizing the acquisitive instinct with the welfare of society as a whole. The utopians sought to achieve this by eradicating it through a communal ownership of property. Some of them sought to bring this about through the enlistment of the sympathies of powerful individuals, a method which is clearly out of harmony with the operation of the law of causality in the world of social relationships. The American method of meeting this basic problem has been largely by means of antitrust legislation. It is accepted as such by the people at large as well as by the political parties. Antitrust legislation seeks to meet the problem in a pragmatic way by preserving the stimulative economic qualities of the acquisitive instinct while eradicating opportunities for its virulent effects, which show themselves in the misuse of the profit motive, through elimination of the antisocial uses of the power which property confers upon individuals.

Income and inheritance taxation, workingmen's compensation, legalization of collective bargaining and of cooperative organizations, to mention only a few instances, reflect the theory that private property should not be used to the detriment of society. And this, in turn, reflects the fundamental democratic principle that the liberty of one individual finds its limits in the liberty of others.

Antitrust legislation does not aproach the fundamental problem of property from the point of view of a deterministic concept of the inevitable revolutionary rearrangement of property relations through the elimination of the institution of private property. It makes a pragmatic approach to this problem as conditioned by the peculiarities of the

American historical development and the resultant cultural attitude of the American people toward their development.

Antitrust legislation has been the American philosophy of economic action. It is native to the American atmosphere, but it is now being confronted with dangers which are undermining its efficacy.

These dangers lie in two directions. First, there are the efforts to render antitrust legislation ineffective through insufficient funds, through pressures on Congress, and through the enactment of legislation exempting certain industries from the operation of the law. Second, there are the dangers through minimizing, often deliberately, the significance of antitrust legislation as it bears on the crucial problem with which this country is faced — that of the concentration of economic power.

Although the problem of monopoly is attracting more and more attention, in most discussions concerning economic problems it is not given a place commensurate with its basic significance. Efforts to make the nation ignore the basic importance of antitrust activities are aided by public apathy in prosperous times and in time of war, when monopolies usually make their greatest advance. And, even in times of depression, the evil of the concentration of economic power does not catch the eye as do prices, wages, working conditions, and similar factors — which are actually secondary to the main problem of competitive opportunities of access to economic resources.

In our democracy legislation is our only means to solve this problem — the crucial problem in the world today — through democratic processes carried on in the light of the American tradition. Failure to meet, through governmental anti-monopoly activities, the challenge of the monopolistic control of the economic resources may render ineffective a conscious control of the social environment. It may lead this country towards a subservience to the blind forces of history. We must remember that these have in other countries fatalistically created a situation under which an equitable access to economic resources could be achieved only through revolutionary upheavals.

So far as America is concerned, despite the action of the economic forces which has brought about the highest degree of concentration in industry and the formation of a great class of industrial and factory workers, the quality which has developed has not been of the revolutionary variety. What has happened, in fact, has been the preservation of the traditional American pragmatic outlook on life working through strong disciplined nationally organized labor unions and not through a militant revolutionary organization. There is always danger, however, that the pressure on the human element by economic forces in the form of a monopolistic concentration of economic power, if un-checked, may prove, in the long run the correctness of the Marxian theory that the economic factor will in the end assert itself.

[1] Gustave Herve, *The Social Movement in Present Day France.*

[2] Samuel E. Morison and Henry S. Commager, *Growth of the American Republic,* Oxford University Press, Vol. II, pp. 271-272.

[3] Horace Kallen, "Pragmatism," *Encyclopedia of the Social Sciences,* Macmillan, pp. 307-308, Vol. XII.

[4] G. W. F. Hegel, *Lectures on the Philosophy of History,* Bell and Daldy York-street, London, 1872, pp. 89-90.

[5] Frederick Jackson Turner, *The Significance of the Frontier in American History,* 1893.

[*] Within recent years Turner's theory of the frontier has been challenged by several writers. Louis N. Hacker in his *Triumph of American Capitalism* accepts this theory with the reservation that the workers in the cities did not take up land; that it was principally the immigrants that avoided the cities and went on the land. Bascially this fact confirms Hegel's and Turner's thesis inasmuch as it led to the same result — more elbow room in the cities. Charles Beard sees the significant factor in our 19th century history in the class struggle. It is difficult to see how separate manifestations of conflicts of interests which undoubtedly occurred during the period can be generalized into a class struggle in view of the opportunities for an independent existence offered by the expanding continent as brought out by Hegel and Turner and brilliantly depicted by Theodore Roosevelt in his *Winning of the West.* As to Harold Laski's "demolition" of Turner's frontier thesis in his *American Democracy,* it seems to be the product of the author's anxiety to demolish the "myth" of American "particularism" probably because it does not fit into the Marxian scheme.

[6] Carl R. Fish, *The Development of American Nationality,* American Book Company, p. 3.

[7] Saul Padover, *Jefferson,* Harcourt, Brace, and Company, p. 54.

[8] Vernon L. Parrington, *Main Currents in American Thought,* Harcourt, Brace, and Company, Book III, Part II, pp. 343-344.

[9] *Ibid.,* p. 344.

[10] Saul Padover, *Jefferson,* Harcourt, Brace, and Company, p. 55.

[11] *Ibid.,* p. 55.

[12] *Ibid.,* p. 56.

[13] Morison and Commager, *The Growth of the American Republic,* Oxford University Press, Vol. I, p. 195.

[14] *Ibid.,* p. 339.

[15] William T. Evjue, "Wisconsin" in *Our Sovereign State,* edited by Robert M. Allen, New York, 1949, p. 230.

[16] John W. McConnell, "The Sociology and Economics of Class Conflict," *American Economic Review,* Papers and Proceedings, May, 1949, pp. 38-39.

[17] *Ibid.,* p. 39.

[18] *Ibid.,* p. 39.

[19] Joyce O. Hertzler, *History of Utopian Thought,* Macmillan, p. 148.

CHAPTER VII

Concentration of Economic Power and
Its Effect on the National Economy

A serious difficulty which confronts the student of the problem of concentration of economic power, lies in the controversy concerning the question of fact, as to whether our economy is competitive or whether competition is stifled by monopoly and monopolistic practices. There are economists who proclaim that the American economy is highly competitive; or who contend that we have not sufficient facts to arrive at definite conclusions concerning the gravity of the monopoly problem in the United States. On the other hand, studies and investigations extending over a number of years show an increasing trend toward the concentration of economic power. Studies by Berle and Means, by the Temporary National Economic Committee, the Twentieth Century Fund, the National Resources Committee, the Smaller War Plants Corporation, the Federal Trade Commission and the Antitrust Division of the U. S. Department of Justice have indicated this trend in a number of ways. Dr. Edward H. Levi cites facts which bring out that "this direction is shown by figures as to percentage of assets controlled, income received and workers employed."[1] The evidence, therefore, substantiates the view that our economy is characterized by a high degree of concentration and restriction of competition.

Referring to Chapter III of the *Modern Corporation and Private Property* by Adolph Berle and Gardiner Means which bears the title "Concentration of Economic Power," David Lynch says: "In that now-famous work of Berle and Means it is shown that substantially all the major production in American industry was carried on under the corporate form of organization. But concentration did not cease there. Not only had the Adam Smith type of individualistic enterpriser all but passed from the scene, but also there was marked concentration even among corporations. Out of more than 300,000 nonfinancial corporations it was found that less than seven-hundredths of one per cent controlled half the corporate wealth. In other words, nearly half of the corporate wealth in the United States is in the control of two hundred corporations."[2]

Centralization of economic activities has led to the gradual elimination of independent business concerns. "There has been a decisive shift in the population toward the category of 'working for others', which is

especially significant in the case of small business men and professional
men, many of whom, rather than entering business on their own account, are becoming employees of large corporations." [3]

But even with respect to the several million businessmen who are
operating, this group of proprietors is undergoing far-reaching
changes. "The locus of economic decisions, of initiative and energy
is being shifted from numerous small centers to a relatively small
number of large units, thereby affecting the entrepreneurial functions traditionally exercised by the small business men. To an increasing extent these functions are being relinquished by the small
business man and transferred to the large units which dominate the
scene. The freedom of action of small business has diminished.
Though the influence of the large concerns varies from industry to
industry, from case to case, quite generally the independence of the
small enterprise is declining." [4]

An important factor in the development of the concentration of
economic power are the activities of the financial interests. In a
report to a Congressional committee relating to the control of industry by financial groups, the Anti-trust Division of the United States
Department of Justice stated that "practically every important industry shows bankers' inclination to merge and combine competing companies." [5] The report quotes from the Smaller War Plants investigation which points out that "ordinary measures of industrial concentration do not in themselves measure the full extent of concentration
of economic power. To the extent that groups of companies are
controlled or influenced by investment bankers, actual concentration
is furthered even more." [6]

In appraising the significance of the activities of the financial
groups with respect to mergers of industries it should be pointed out
that such mergers are not brought into being for purposes of greater
efficiency — the standard excuse of monopolistic combinations. What
the investment bankers are primarily interested in is the sale of
securities. Whether a given merger is an economic necessity, or at
least presents economic progress, is of little consequence to them.
What they want is a wide base for the floating of securities. Mergers
and combinations, which are among "the most prolific sources of new
security issues," [7] represent a wider and more secure base than two
or three companies, "each one of them too small or too closely held
to be a source of security selling business." [8]

According to the Antitrust Division's report, "these mergers and
consolidations have many advantages from the point of view of the
investment banker. First of all they create a new and much larger

security issue for them to market than would otherwise be available; second, in the process of recapitalizing the combined assets of the old companies, the banker may have an opportunity to secure a substantial interest in the new and larger company; and, third, they frequently manage to place themselves on the board of directors of the newly created company." [9]

As directors, the investment bankers, because of the nature of their business, are bound to be an influence against competition. "In the marketing of securities bankers usually form large underwriter syndicates. As a general practice, they participate in one another's syndicates. Thus, it is not unusual for the investment banker who is represented on the board of directors of one steel company to be active in the sales of a competing steel company's securities. These ties in the banker's major field of activity, securities merchandising, cannot help but restrict seriously his interest in competition as a company director. The friendly relations with other investment bankers are more valuable to them than the expansion of a particular company as a result of successful competition against other companies in the same field." [10]

An outstanding historical example of combinations brought about by investment bankers was the formation of the United States Steel Corporation at the beginning of the century. "The banking firm of J. P. Morgan was instrumental at that time in bringing together a number of steel companies to form one of the earliest corporate giants of American industry. In order to survive, some of the small units in the industry also had to combine; the consequence was a further reduction of the area of competition in this industry. Other industries, such as chemicals, building materials, other metals, and even bread baking and milk distribution have experienced the same sort of development. In all of these cases investment bankers played a very powerful role in bringing together and combining competing companies." [11]

There are very few industries in which one concern has an exclusive control. The usual pattern is domination by three or four concerns. This, however, with few exceptions, does not bring about conditions conducive to private competition between monopolies in any appreciable degree. It even strengthens control, through the apportionment of power, looking towards the elimination of risks which would threaten the profits and the investments of the several concerns if they were to compete with each other and run the hazard of inviting competition.

The Temporary National Economic Committee points out that the "high degree of concentration of ownership must be regarded as the *minimum* measure of control over the 200 largest non-financial American corporations. There are numerous ways in which control over corporations can be exercised other than through direct stock ownership. Some of these instruments of control are proxy machinery, interlocking directorates, investment trusts, banking affiliations, etc. It is principally through these more indirect methods that the great financial interests of the country — the Morgans, Mellons, du Ponts, etc. — really exercise most of their tremendous power and control." [12]

The powerful indirect control vested in the great corporations, combined with the momentum acquired by concentrated economic power, overrides all the analyses which aim at the determination of the degree of monopolization in various fields and attempts to determine at any given time the respective areas of competition and monopoly in our industry.

The Effects of the Concentration of Economic Power

Concentrated economic power presents, as was noted, a problem of basic importance in that it affects opportunities for competitive access to economic resources. Human society has no other choice than to live off the resources which are provided by its physical environment through the medium of farms, mines and quarries, factories and industrial plants. It is a simple truth that if the ownership of economic resources is monopolized by a few, the rest of society is compelled to pay tribute to the owners of these resources. In an agrarian economy where land is the principal economic resource this tribute is in the form of an exorbitant part of its labor. In a modern industrial economy this tribute is in the form of unemployment, depressions and high prices for goods. The antisocial character of the concentration of private economic power is that it interferes with competitive access to economic resources, and with access to the abundance of material goods and services made possible by the progress of technology.

Physical access to material resources refers to their availability in a natural, processed or manufactured form. Their economic availability is the relation between prices and purchasing power. A normal relation between these two factors is supposed to be maintained in a competitive society by the free play of competition. Interference with competition upsets the normal relations between prices and purchasing power by leading to artificial prices which weaken the consumer's buying ability and reduce the economic availability of commodities.

In normal times, under normal historical conditions, in a country like ours with its enormous productive capacity, artificial prices are generally the result of some form of concerted monopolistic control. They imply a discretionary control, unified or concerted, of the price at which goods can be obtained. Since, however, goods are the end results of production, the discretionary control of the price as it refers to goods is largely an illusion. It presupposes a discretionary control of the means of production, and in certain cases — notably in the present commercial type of agriculture — a control over distributive facilities.

Monopolistic control of the means of production leads to the limitation of production. The average entrepreneur fears an abundance of goods. His greatest concern is not to take risks with his investment. If he has any measure of control over production — either alone or in concert with others, whether of an open or a clandestine nature — he will strive to obtain as high profits as possible from limited production. He will avoid venturing into the dark forest of uncertain demand, possibility of sharp competition, and other dread spirits that infest the world of business and threaten profits and investments.

"No monopoly can maintain its control over prices in the face of a surplus which it does not control. . . . The evil of monopoly is not its size; it is its power to hold back production, thus to exploit unorganized business, consumers and farmers." [13]

Thurman Arnold points out that "the four horsemen, fixed prices, low turnover, restricted production, and monopoly control have ridden through our economy from factory to farm." He quotes from the London Economist which, describing England's failure to produce before the fall of France in 1940, referred to these restrictive practices as follows: "It is a set of ideas that is admirable for obtaining security, 'orderly development' and remunerative profits for those already established in the industry — at the cost of an irreducible body of general unemployment. It is emphatically not a set of ideas that can be expected to yield the maximum of production, or to give the country wealth in peace and strength in war." [14]

Arnold cites the example of the corporation controlling zinc, which, during the first world war, "refused to license new producers except on condition that they go out of business after the war." [15] He mentions the case of a corporation, having a practical monopoly of an important basic metal, which offered a contract to the government during the war. This contract "provided that whenever the price of the metal fell to a figure considered unreasonably low, the corporation should have the power to shut down production in the government plant, and at the same time keep control of the plant so that no one else could produce." [16]

An illuminating instance of how threats to profits and investment affect business thinking is contained in the record of the Special Committee to Study Problems of American Small Business, in the hearings of the steel sub-committee. At these hearings Walter Reuther, President of the United Automobile Workers of America (C.I.O.), took issue with the representatives of the steel industry concerning plans to reduce output by 20 per cent in 1947, on the ground that, considering the basic importance of steel in our economy, such a reduction would mean widespread unemployment by 1950.[17] He stated that the testimony of the representatives of the steel industry showed that they believed that "their chances of achieving full employment were too risky to justify the capital investment in steel making which full employmen will require." [18]

The moving force of capitalism is the profit motive. Upon the way this functions depends the success or failure of the capitalist system. As envisioned by Adam Smith, in the conditions of free competition, it was destined to play a beneficent social role as an incentive to production; as it actually turned out, under the monopolization of productive facilities, it has been diverted to the protection of profits and investments at the expense of full production. Its misuse has become an antisocial force which, by restricting the competitive access to economic resources, leads to economic inequity. This inequity is, in turn, reflected in a maldistribution of incomes which is generally accepted as the basic cause of economic maladjustments.

Referring to the fact that the Sherman Antitrust Law has been applied throughout most of its history against abuses rather than against monopolies, Dean Edward H. Levi of the University of Chicago Law School states that "this has permitted an enormous and growing amount of concentration in economic power" and that "it has permitted two great merger movements — each of which ended in a depression." [19]

Monopoly and Economic Inequity

The strategic position occupied by the monopolist gives him the power not to pass on to labor in higher wages, or to consumers in lower prices, the gains resulting from technological improvements.

"The monopolist's price will almost always be above the one that he would charge if he were under the necessity of meeting competition. His freedom from competitive or regulatory restraints enables him to obtain a profit much larger than that required to enlist his services in the administration of industrial activity. Enterprises which monopolize important fields are almost invariably corporate in form. Their net income, insofar as it is not reinvested in plant and equipment, declared as dividends on preferred shares, or diverted to insiders, goes to the holders of their common stock. Declaration of dividends on common stock thus represents a distribution of profits of monopoly. If this stock were widely held, monopoly would still operate to impair the general standard of living, but it would not accentuate inequality. But the ownership of all corporate stock in concentrated and corporate dividends goes mainly to the rich. In 1929, more than 83 per cent of all the dividends paid to individuals went to the 3.28 per cent of the population who filed income tax returns; 78 per cent of them went to the richest three-tenths of one per cent. Concentration in the distribution of dividends derived from monopoly is at least as great.

"Monopoly thus makes for economic inequality. The laborers whose incomes may be limited by the monopolist's failure to pay wages equal to their productivity are numerous. The producers of materials whose incomes are depressed by the low prices that the monopolist sometimes pays may also be numerous. The consumers whose real incomes are reduced by the high prices that the monopolist charges are likewise numerous. The stockholders who share the unnecessarily high profits that the monopolist thus obtains are few in number. A more nearly perfect mechanism for making the poor poorer and the rich richer could scarcely be devised." [20]

As a consequence there is a tremendous discrepancy in normal times in the incomes of the various population groups. In the year 1939, which represents a normal year, "eight million families in the United States faced starvation on incomes of less than $750 a year, and another eleven million families were described as fighting poverty on 'incomes between $750 and $1,500'." [21] This suggests that these families had almost no access to economic resources.

Accessibility to economic resources is thus curtailed in the modern economy in two ways: directly, through restrictions of production to protect profits and investments; and indirectly, through the monetary tribute which the worker and the consumer pay to the monopolist. The latter likewise reduces production, because of the curtailment in mass demand for products resulting from the decrease in purchasing power consequent upon lower wages and higher prices for commodities. "The central economic problem is . . . the conversion of a high potential power to consume into an actual power to consume: a wider distribution of progress." [22]

Capacity production is conditioned upon accessibility to economic resources. Only full employment and decent earnings show that opportunities of access to economic resources are equitably distributed; that is they show that all those who are willing and able to work are afforded opportunities to utilize these resources through work on farms and in the mines or through employment in factories and industrial plants.

The normal function of the national economy requires capacity production. The lack of a full utilization of productive facilities, which is the direct consequence of the monopolization of access to economic resources, creates conditions for the development of crises and depressions. Planned scarcity production places a barrier between the people and the economic resources.

"For years, our economic system and that of the British had been overwhelmingly concerned with preserving the security and the income of established and dominant groups. These groups stifled new productive enterprise in order to protect themselves against competition. They limited their own output to prevent what they called 'a surplus'. They failed to expand their productive capacity because they feared expansion might lead to future competition or future surplus. They were afraid of industrial plenty, which alone can give a nation wealth in peace or strength in war." [23]

Monopoly thus evolves a regulatory power which is less concerned with production in the public interest than with the idea of avoiding risks. The more an economy is based on concentrated large scale enterprises, the more serious is the problem of risks. If such enterprises are, because of their size or some other strategic factor, vested with the power of monopoly, the regulatory function of free competition is replaced by the regulatory function of an arbitrary authority. This authority is guided primarily by the idea of taking as little risk as possible, regardless of the consideration of public welfare. It is such a policy, as well as the thought underlying it, that was formulated by the steel industry when it decided to reduce steel production in 1947.

Restricting industrial production to safeguard profits is of an especially critical significance to agriculture inasmuch as farm prices undergo considerable fluctuations with any reduction in demand, while industrial prices are "administered" in the sense that they are fixed through an adjustment of production to decreasing demand which prevents appreciable price fluctuations.

The ability of the industry to maintain prices out of proportion to changes in production was brought out by Secretary of Agriculture

Charles F. Brannan in the course of a hearing before a House committee concerned with the monopoly problem.[24] Mr. Brannan cited concrete statistics to show the disparity between the considerable decrease in production and the comparatively small decrease in industrial prices in certain industries between 1929 and the depression low of the 30's:

"Agricultural implement prices declined 14 per cent, payrolls declined 83 per cent; iron and steel prices went down 16 per cent, payrolls went down 75 per cent; cement prices went down 13 per cent, payrolls 72 per cent; aluminum prices went down 21 per cent, payrolls 69 per cent."[25]

Mr. Brannan also pointed out: "At the same time farm prices went down by two-thirds and in self-protection many farmers increased their crop acreages. From 1932 to 1938 industrial production averaged about 25 per cent below that of 1929 while farm production averaged approximately the same as in 1929."[26]

Looking at more up-to-date figures, he added: "Since the end of 1947 the prices of farm machinery have gone up 20 per cent and other farm equipment and supplies have gone up nearly 10 per cent. But prices received by farmers for their commodities have dropped 18 per cent."[27]

From this data Mr. Brannan drew this conclusion: "The interests of the farmer and the general public require eternal vigilance against monopolistic prices and other improper and undesirable uses of concentrated economic power."[28]

It is the problem of the domination of restrictive practices which appear either directly as monopolistic controls or indirectly as various forms of tacit or open understanding between large producers that is implied in our antitrust legislation. While it is true that "there is confusion in our anti-monopoly tradition in that we do not know whether we are opposed to size or merely to unreasonably high prices,"[29] still there is a widespread feeling that the power which results from size leads to the subordination of public welfare to private interests. The reality of the power of size has been recognized within the past few years by the courts in the Pullman and the Alcoa cases.

Considering that free competition is the essence of the economic ideal of American democracy, the extent to which monopoly has developed in this country is indicative of the effective working of a compelling force of an anticompetitive character.

The functioning of the capitalism of free enterprise rests on the concept of profit as regulating automatically our economic relationships in the direction of free competition. Monopoly and monopolistic practices imply the misuse of the profit motive, inasmuch as they eliminate or restrain free competition. As a conseqeunce, profits resulting from monopoly do not serve the interests of the American nation as a whole. The misuse of the concept of profit weakens the incentive towards a full utilization of productive facilities, the end and purpose of man's struggle with nature. It eliminates competition which, in a capitalist economy, is considered as the basic prerequisite of an effective public control of the social environment.

A report of the Antitrust Division of the U. S. Department of Justice to a Committee of the House of Representatives calls attention to the fact that "the monopoly problem in American industry is today more serious and widespread than at any time since the passage of the Sherman Act" and that "the most serious consequence of concentration, as it confronts the nation at the present time, is that is severely restricts that freedom of economic opportunity which is a basic principle of the American system of government." [30]

The present status of the concentration of economic power in this country and the threat it presents to a free economy are graphically brought out in a summary of the report of the Antitrust Division of the U. S. Department of Justice to the above-mentioned monopoly sub-committee. The forms and methods "by which monopoly groups today are seeking to establish and perpetuate control" are summarized by the Antitrust Division as follows: [31]

"1. Monopolistic control is generally based upon one or more of the following elements:

"(a) Control of most available sources of raw materials,

"(b) Control of technology, research and know-how obtained in large part through an ever increasing concentration of ownership or control over the facilities necessary to conduct industrial research,

"(c) Control of the channels and the methods of distribution in the market. A whole array of ingenious devices has been employed in numerous industries to determine who may enter the market, what shall be produced, how markets shall be divided, and what quantities of products may be bought or sold. The monopoly methods most often employed for the purposes of such market control include: direct-marketing agreements which divided markets nationally and inter-nationally into non-competitive zones; price-fixing agreements; the use of standardized cost systems, standardized price data and trade statis-tics; organized discrimination with respect to particular classes of in-dustrial as well as individual buyers and sellers; basing-point systems by which prices are closely administered in a number of market areas; and restrictive patent licensing.

"(d) Division of fields of production and research among powerful monopoly groups in closely related branches of industry. In this, groups of restraints are found: most of the major abuses used in the administration of patents; attempts to pervert scientific research in order to maintain artificial price structures; attempts to dictate the processes that may be used in the manufacture, the raw materials that may be purchased and in some instances, the customers to whom products may be sold as well as the terms of sale; and,

"(e) Increasing concentration of control over credit resources and of relative financial power in many industries as compared with the resources available to small independent enterprise.

"2. It has been among the primary aims of powerful monopoly groups to control dynamic sectors of technology and to prevent the emergence of competitive enterprise in such important areas as chemistry, electronics, light metals, pharmaceutical products, and other industries which hold the greatest promise for the creation of new products, new services and new types of employment and investment. The maintenance of the American industrial leadership in the world economy largely depends on the scope and speed with which new technological resources are utilized. Competition and the development of independent enterprise constitute the central means of achieving these objectives. Continued monopoly domination, therefore, seriously endangers the preeminence of this country in industrial research and threatens to retard the pace of needed development.

"3. Evidence accumulated within recent years demonstrates conclusively that monopoly groups and techniques of monopoly control have seriously affected this country's foreign commerce. In particular cartel agreements between monopoly groups in the United States and the powerful industrial combines abroad have restricted the exports of numerous products of American industry to various market areas throughout the world. At the same time, imports of many materials, essential to the operation of American industry, have been strictly limited by agreement among monopoly groups here and sold abroad.

"4. Evidence compiled in antitrust actions instituted against cartels and monopolies discloses that the access of American industry to strategic sectors of technology and to critical materials has, in many cases been restricted or even closed through cartel agreements. In some instances limitations have been placed upon our capacity to produce materials necessary to the military security and economic welfare of the United States. The introduction and expansion of new processes and new industries have at times been delayed, or even completely prevented under the terms of monopoly agreements because of monopolistic control of processes, patents, price structures, and markets.

"5. Studies recently compiled by other government agencies emphasize that the relative growth of monopoly was accelerated during the years of World War II with a corresponding unavoidable decline in competition."

In conclusion, the report states that, in "terms of the maintenance of free enterprise the monopoly problem constitutes the greatest challenge of our time. The problem is to preserve our ideals of independence of spirit and freedom of enterprise against the encroachment of monopoly control into almost every important realm of our economic life." [32]

That monopoly, whatever its degree or aspects, is a fact is attested by evidence. It is true that a complete monopoly by one concern rarely occurs in this country, if at all. But duopoly or oligopoly have the same effect as complete monopoly. Referring to a situation where competitive forces do not operate, Mr. Bergson states: "Where you have a situation of that kind, and you are most likely to have it in a monopoly industry or an oligopoly industry, then you have monopoly power whether it is in the hands of the one or in the hands of the four or three or the two." [33] Many of our important industries are controlled by a limited number of concerns.

Emphasis on incomplete monopoly and "incomplete" competition tends to minimize the seriousness of the problem of monopoly as do references to isolated examples of competition in the automobile industry, for example. But a deterrent of even more serious consequences to our efforts to contend with this problem are deceitful appearances which play a basic role in the halting progress of society towards equitable social relationships.

Inflation epitomizes the absence of competitive accessibilities to economic resources. Considering the technological efficiency of our industry and our wealth in economic resources it is to be traced in the last analysis to restrictions which prevent the full utilization of our resources.

The significance of monopoly is associated with its injurious effects on the economic life of the nation. A surface prosperity at times, however, conceals the baneful effect of monopolies. The general prosperity of the twenties made us overlook the action of the monopolistic forces which led to the depression of the thirties and exposed the illusory character of that prosperity.

Illusory periods of prosperity are usually revealed in inflation — i.e., in a disproportion between incomes and living costs.

"'Inflation, though pleasant for some people, hurts those whose dollar incomes do not increase or increase less than living costs; and also sharpens conflicts of economic interests and impairs the group consensus necessary for solving national problems." [34]

The nature of monopoly as a barrier to the competitive and, hence, the fullest utilization of economic resources to meet the needs of our economy was distinctly revealed in a statement issued by Congressman Emanuel Celler in connection with the question of steel production for mobilization purposes. In this statement the Congressman, who is chairman of the Committee on the Judiciary of the House of Representatives and who also heads the Subcommittee on the Study of Monopoly Power, dispels the illusion that "defense requirements have caused the steel shortage" and brings out that the shortage of steel is "'chronic and national in scope." He points out that "defense needs have illuminated the situation that as long as the industry is dominated by United States Steel, competition cannot work to provide adequate supplies."

Says Congressman Celler:

"This shortage [of steel] demonstrates why there must be vigorous enforcement of antitrust laws to protect the public against the abuse of monopoly power, whether exercised by one company or a group acting in concert. . . .

"The recent investigation by the subcommittee on Study of the Monopoly Power disclosed that the steel industry of this country is too small because the presence of a company as large as United States Steel in the industry has stifled competition and expansion of capacity by its policies of domination. *The report of the experts retained by the United States Steel Corporation, indicates expansion and efficiency alike have been retarded by policies rooted in inertia, fear of competition, and fear of progress.* [Italics supplied.]

"It is entirely misleading to assert . . . that current defense requirements have caused the steel shortage. The shortage of steel which occasions profound concern among manufacturers, consumers, and those responsible for the nation's security, is chronic and national in scope. Defense needs have illuminated the situation that as long as the industry is dominated by United States Steel, competition cannot work to provide adequate supplies.

"This situation is not new. It should be remembered that time and again representatives of the leading steel producers have assured the public that steel capacity was adequate. Repeatedly, these assurances have been shown to be hollow hopes, voiced to forestall vigorous expansion.

"The little businessman who is rationed out of the market whenever steel supply is tight, the large industry which is forced to use substitutes

or limit output, and the national defense program which must cope
with continued scarcity of this vital material — all suffer from the son-
sequences of policies which produce shortage. These policies have
their source in monopolistic thinking, and result in gray markets.
These are not the qualities of progressive, competitive industry, and
the nation has come to see the fallacy of the pretense that the industry
can do the job required as long as its policies are guided by a philosophy of artificial scarcity on the part of its leaders. It is the same
philosophy, it may be said which cut employment and production
rather than prices in the depression of the thirties." [35]

In concluding his statement, Congressman Celler affirms that "national security and the public interest are alike endangered if the steel
industry is held back by reluctant policies toward expansion."

In an address delivered to the national convention of the Congress
of Industrial Organizations (C.I.O.), on November 23, 1950, Secretary
of the Interior Oscar Chapman stated that "a mounting steel shortage
. . . was endangering the country's future." He blamed "a few 'short-
sighted' men who he said have refused to expand steel production
capacity." [36]

In conclusion, it should be brought out that probably the worst instance of lack of competitive accessibility to economic resources resulting from restrictive monopolistic practices is presented by the
shortage of housing.

[1] Edward H. Levi, "The Antitrust Laws and Monopoly," *University of Chicago Law Review*, February 1947, p. 164.
[2] David Lynch, *The Concentration of Economic Power*, Columbia University Press, 1946, pp. 10-11.
[3] *Economic Concentration and World War II*, report of Smaller War Plants Corporation to the Special Committee to Study Problems of American Small Business, U. S. Senate, p. 14.
[4] Kurt Mayer, "Small Business as a Social Institution," *Social Research*, September 1947, pp. 343-44.
[5] *United States Versus Economic Concentration and Monopoly*. A staff report to the Monopoly subcommittee on Small Business of the House of Representatives, Washington, 1946, p. 239.
[6] *Ibid.*, p. 38.
[7] *Ibid.*, p. 239.
[8] *Ibid.*, p. 239.
[9] *Ibid.*, p. 239.
[10] *Ibid.*, p. 239
[11] *Ibid.*, p. 239.
[12] *Economic Concentration and World War II*, report of the Smaller War Plants Corporation to the Special Committee to Study Problems of American Small Business, U. S. Senate, p. 16.
[13] Thurman Arnold, *Democracy and Free Enterprise*, University of Oklahoma Press, 1942, p. 24.
[14] *Ibid.*, p. 17.
[15] *Ibid.*, p. 18.
[16] *Ibid.*, p. 20.

[17] "One Hunded Million Tons of Steel," statement filed by Walter P. Reuther, *Hearings of the Steel Subcommittee of the Special Committee to Study Problems of American Small Business*, U. S. Senate, July 21, 1947.

[18] *Ibid.*

[19] Edward H. Levi, "The Antitrust Laws and Monopoly," *University of Chicago Law Review*, February, 1947, p. 183.

[20] Clair Wilcox, *Competition and Monopoly in American Industry*, pp. 17-18.

[21] David Lynch, *The Concentration of Economic Power*, p. 249.

[22] David Lynch, *The Concentration of Economic Power*, Columbia University Press, 1946, p. 251; quoted from "U.S. Industrialization," *Fortune*, February, 1940, p. 50.

[23] Thurman Arnold, *Democracy and Free Enterprise*, University of Oklahoma Press, p. 34.

[24] *Study of Monopoly Power*, hearings before the subcommittee on Study of Monopoly Power of the Committee on the Judiciary; House of Representatives, 81st Congress, First Session, Serial No. 14, Part 1; p. 169.

[25] *Ibid.*, p. 169.

[26] *Ibid.*, p. 169.

[27] *Ibid.*, p. 169.

[28] *Ibid.*, p. 169.

[29] Edward H. Levi, "The Antitrust Laws and Monopoly," *The University of Chicago Law Review*, February 1947, p. 153.

[30] *United States versus Economic Concentration and Monopoly*, report of the Monopoly Subcommittee on Small Business, House of Representatives, 79th Congress, p. 34.

[31] *United States Versus Economic Concentration and Monopoly*, Report to the Monopoly subcommittee of the Committee on Small Business, House of Representatives, Washington, 1946, pp. 210-211.

[32] *Ibid.*, pp. 210-211.

[33] Testimony of Assistant Attorney General of the United States, Hearings before the Subcommittee on the study of Monopoly Power; 81st Congress, p. 367.

[34] "The Problem of Economic Stability," report of the Committee of the American Economic Association, *The American Economic Review*, September 1950, p. 506.

[35] Statement of Representative Emanuel Celler, press release, October 26, 1950.

[36] *Wisconsin State Journal*, November 24, 1950.

CHAPTER VIII

Types of Monopoly Practice

The facts uncovered by the investigations of the National Temporary Economic Committee were of a special value in that they brought to the public consciousness the many and varied practices which in various subtle ways serve to implement monopoly without resorting to the old crude ways of destroying competition. A study of these methods shows the resourcefulness which an irrepressible inclination to misuse the profit motive engenders.

David Lynch, in his analysis of the methods of monopoly implementation as they were revealed by the testimony before the Temporar National Economic Committee, states that "the ways of monopoly are protean; monopolists are less concerned with methods than with results. If one instrument is outlawed, or for some practical purpose fails to produce the desired result, others are employed."[1] No sharp boundary lines exist. "Different methods may be employed at the same time to achieve the same ends; and their operations may so overlap and intertwine as to make them indistinguishable — merely different aspects of the same method."[2]

These methods of monopoly implementation are in many cases "subtle and intangible alliances and understandings unrecognized by the consuming public and unreached by monopoly laws."[3] These alliances and understandings have replaced the trust activities of former years which were frankly and crudely illegal. Basically, however, they are the direct successors of those methods and represent only polite variations in form without change in substance.

As the testimony presented at the hearings of the Temporary National Economic Committee shows, these methods have had a considerable effect on consolidating and expanding monopoly domination under its varied forms. The pressing danger of these methods — in addition to the concrete results of their application to business relationships — is that many of them create an illusion of innocence of any violation of the principles involved in free competition. Collectively, the recent methods represent a newer form of promoting that misuse of the profit motive which has been forcing on the country the domination of concerted economic power in defiance of law, tradition, and national wishes and aspirations. As in the case of the older methods of monopoly formation, there is an irrepressible drive, whenever opportunity affords, to turn the profit motive into an instrument of private economic power instead of letting it fulfill its functions as a carrier of free competition.

In its early history the misuse of the profit motive showed itself in a cold and openly unscrupulous manner; it aimed at forming a solid foundation for the private domination of our economy. This was toward the last decade of the past century, at the time of the tobacco monopoly, of steel rail pools, of railroad rate discriminations and of the far-flung competition-crushing tactics of the Standard Oil Company. The general pattern followed, after deciding upon the fate of a competing oil company, was "to drop the price of oil products — largely kerosene at that time — to a level in the competitor's restricted locality which would quickly bring him to terms. If the local producer refused to go along, consumers in a limited area were given the kerosene free or at a nominal sum until the price was patched up." [4]

Such earlier methods of monopoly formation, although still used to some extent, have given way to tactics, no more ethical but merely less glaring and conspicuous, which are just as effective in thwarting anti-monopoly legislation since they are merely different phases of monopoly domination, involving as they do some subtle form of concerted action. Among the many methods which were brought to the attention of the national Temporary Economic Committee the three outstanding examples are: price leadership, the basing point system, and the trade associations.

Price Leadership as an Intangible Form of Monopolistic Combination

David Lynch refers to price leadership as a type of monopolistic combination in which, "unlike the trust, the pool, the holding company and other methods of combination prevalent at the turn of the century", it is "inconspicuous and offers little tangible evidence of collusion and conspiracy despite the obviousness of its results. It often represents nothing more than a tacit understanding among producers to 'follow the leader' in price policy." [5]

According to George P. Comer, "price leadership" and "market leadership" constitute "one of the most important parts of the new trust problem today." [6] This means that in a field "in which there are a few important producers in an industry, no one of which is necessarily dominant from the point of view of volume of production, all the producers both large and small are likely to pattern after the leaders in price policies, price quotations and marketing methods. "Under price leadership, price control of a particular industry may be as rigid as in the days of the old pools and later the trusts and still later the corporate form of consolidation." [7]

In its simplest form the market leader is a dominant concern which sets the price of its products, usually with the certainty that other producers will immediately follow the quotations whether the trend is upward or downward. Almost every form of marketing activity in many industries is dominated by the leadership principle. "Though relatively unknown a few decades ago, price leadership was described to the TNEC as one of the most dominant of prevalent types of monopoly" with the statement that "prices determined under the price leadership regime probably constitute the most common form of controlled prices in the American market." [8]

Those, then, are the primary facts concerning a highly effective form of combination. That it is widespread in American industry and that it is interfering with the free play of competitive forces has been substantiated by authoritative studies and investigations, notably the work of the Temporary National Economic Committee. Such a wealth of data is obtainable on this subject and so much of it is analyzed in such a compelling and penetrating manner — to cite as an outstanding instance Mr. David Lynch's work in this field — that nothing could be added by reciting over again the pertinent facts and analyzing them anew in the light of the monopoly problem. What is of interest with respect to our discussion is to study how price leadership and the other more recent and sophisticated methods of monopoly implementation serve as tools of the misuse of the profit motive. For, as was noted previously, this misuse plays an effective role in doing away with the institution of competitive enterprise. On this elemental force — misuse of the profit motive — rests the action of two simple commonplace factors, the interplay of which, nonetheless, imparts a momentous significance to the problem of growing concentration of private economic power in this country and the consequent problem of access to economic resources. These two factors are the lure of profits to the strong and the fear of the weaker members of the community that they will be squeezed out of business.

A conspicuous example of the interaction of these two factors was furnished by the data presented in the testimony before the National Temporary Economic Committee. This showed that weaker firms, afraid to jeopardize their business, followed the policies of a powerful concern which dominated the field. Also, "instances have occurred in which militant and aggressive producers in a given field have employed duress to whip competitors into a price leadership program." [9]

Two variations of the interaction of the lure of profits and the fear of being squeezed out of the market are found in situations in which the various interests are of equal strength. In such cases price leadership sometimes results from an unwritten agreement among the parties, arrived at after deliberation and consultation. A similar situation obtains when there are a few giant firms of approximately equal strength each with a healthy respect for the power of the others and each reluctant to engage the others in all-out competition. This situation results in agreement on a price which reveals the desire to "live-and-let-live" as applied to a limited number of business interests in a given market — though not to the consuming public.

Despite the fact that prices determined under the price leadership system are definitely controlled prices, and, as such, violate the elementary capitalistic principle of the determination of prices through the free play of competition, this widespread method of price control is not practiced with secrecy; its existence is not denied by those who adhere to it. Not only is it not concealed but it is discussed openly and without reserve as is shown by testimony before the TNEC. A corporation president said, "We generally make the prices." [10] Another stated: "I was very glad . . . of the opportunity to follow the corporation lead." [11] Others testified that they never initiated price changes but that their custom was to meet these and to follow a policy of "live-and-let-live." One executive stated, "We are too small to lead;" [12] while another merely said, "We have to follow." [13] An industrialist testified that price leadership had been an established practice in his industry as far back as he could remember, and added, "It is the custom of the industry. We have always done it." [14]

Here we have a group of industrialists, business men and executives, all of whom are undoubtedly loyal American citizens whose devotion to the free enterprise system is such that they are ready to throw their full support into a war against an ideology that threatens interference with free competition. And yet these same men do not hesitate to acknowledge openly that they violate the principle of free enterprise by following a practice which constitutes a flagrant denial of the principle of free competition. Considering its prevalence, they apparently do not realize that their practice is turning the American economy into a privately controlled institution.

The influence of the elemental force which is driving these men to act in their business affairs in a spirit directly opposite to that which animates them as American citizens, reaches its climax in those who are conscious that price determination through price leadership is a violation of the spirit and the purpose of anti-monopoly laws and that it constitutes a deliberate method of circumventing those laws.

A consciousness of the violation of these statutes, coupled with a determination to escape censure, is vividly revealed for example, in instructions sent by its executives to the members of the National Association of Petroleum Retailers. The letter containing these instructions was presented to the Temporary National Economic Committee. It described the operations of price leadership. It set forth the intent to initiate a series of price increases for retail gasoline, and outlines the method by which uniform increased prices might be obtained. It referred to the methods used by distributors and proposed to follow their example: "The answer has been before our eyes for many years. . . . In each territory there has been a supplier that was recognized as the market leader. . . . The leader must be a petroleum retailer and he must be followed by all the other retailers in the territory." [15]

That the writer was conscious that what he was suggesting was a method of price control and that the aim and purpose of the policy proposed was concert, collusion, and "conspiracy against the public" is clear from the fact that he warned the members of the trade association against creating any tangible evidence of a price-fixing scheme: "By this time you should be in a position to select your 'market leader' who has the courage and those qualities of leadership that others recognize, and will follow. After he is selected, give him your wholehearted support. Remember not to agree upon a price, but each individual has the right to determine what he wants to do and to announce it, thus avoiding any conspiracy. Your 'market leader' can set a price and the organization can send out a notice." [16]

In industries where one producer is predominantly stronger than the rest, he is often able to lead the industry to a monopolistic control of prices, without the necessity of clandestine agreement or collusion. According to testimony before the TNEC such a predominant position in the beryllium industry, as an instance, was enjoyed by the American Brass Company. When it raised its prices, smaller firms raised theirs identically and simultaneously; when it lowered its prices, smaller firms did likewise. The American Brass Company regularly sent a copy of all new price lists to competitors at the same time that the prices were announced to customers. It is evident from the testimony that the parties concerned complied readily with the implied instructions.

The president of the smallest competing firm — a one and one-half million dollar industry — testified that price leadership was a well crystallized practice and that it "has been the custom of the industry for years on end." [17] This is substantiated by the Hearings before the

Temporary National Economic Committee and is revealed in the following excerpt from the Hearings. What is especially noteworthy is that this excerpt also contains testimony pointing to the consequences of price leadership as it affects the freedom of choice based on individual judgment which is considered as the cornerstone of the free enterprise system.

After Mr. Randall, the president of the firm referred to above, testified that his organization followed the prices announced by the American Brass Company — and that they reduced or increased the price even if they did not have to, in order to be in line with the American Brass Company — the following colloquy took place:[18]

Mr. Cox: "I will put this question to you, Mr. Randall. Why didn't you reduce the price of the fabricated product following that decrease in the price of the master alloy?"

Mr. Randall: "Well, of course I would not make a reduction in the base price of beryllium copper unless the American Brass made a price reduction in beryllium copper."

Mr. Arnold: "You exercise no individual judgment as to the price you charge for your products, then, in a situation?"

Mr. Randall: "Well, I think that is about what it amounts to."

Mr. Arnold: "In other words, the situation is such that you can't pay any attention to the price of the raw material in fixing the prices."

Mr. Randall: "Of course, as Mr. Cox first stated, the industry is one of price leadership, and a small company like ours, making less than 1½ per cent of the total, we have to follow; and I think we have a statement of our price policy here which would perhaps clear that up a little."

Mr. Arnold: "When you say you have to follow, you do not mean anybody told you you had to follow?"

Mr. Randall: "No sir; I don't mean that at all."

Mr. Arnold: "But you have a feeling that something might happen if you didn't."

Mr. Randall: "I do not know what would happen."

Mr. Cox: "You do not want to find out, do you?"

The Chairman: "Well, as a matter of fact, Mr. Randall, if the American Brass Company raised the price would the Brass Company consult you about raising it?"

Mr. Randall: "No sir; not at all."

The Chairman: "You would, however, follow them without exercising any independent judgment as to whether or not it was desirable."

Mr. Randall: "That is correct."

The statement mentioned by Mr. Randall described his company's price policy as follows: "The price schedules issued by the Riverside Metal Company are contingent upon the prices published by the larger units of the industry. From time to time these larger units publish their scale of prices, and our company has no alternative except to meet such published price in order to compete." [19] Mr. Lynch points out that "this statement is characteristic of many statements in the TNEC Hearings in which industrialists speak glibly of meeting competition when describing situations in which competition has been solved by destroying it." [20] He also mentions that at this stage of the hearings a committee member aptly paraphrased the Riverside Metal Company's statement, cited above, as follows: "Our company has no alternative except to meet such published prices in order *not* to compete." [21]

This situation brings out strikingly the working of that elemental anti-competitive force, the misuse of the profit motive, of which price leadership is a conspicuous manifestation. The fatalistic nature of this force is caused by the fear originating in the feeling of insecurity generated by mistrust of competition. The strange, unnatural feature of this is, that fear of competition determines the prices in an economic system supposedly based on competition — a system, too, the competitive character of which is supposed to be safeguarded by proper legislation.

The most vulnerable spot in the totalitarian regimes exposed to democratic criticism is the one-party system and the presentation of a single slate at elections. The obvious defect of such a practice from a democratic point of view is that it does not allow for an opportunity for individual judgment, a situation which results from the lack of alternative opportunities. Opportunity for the exercise of individual judgment is, then, the basic factor in determining whether or not there is democratic freedom. In the case of the freedom of speech, of the freedom of the press and of conscience, it is the possibility of using one's own judgment as to what one ought to say, publish, or believe, without restrictions or fear of punishment that makes for real democracy. The philosophy of free enterprise working through free competition gives a definite impulse to economic democracy, inasmuch as it allows free play for the use of judgment in the economic sphere.

But whether in a straight out-and-out merger or in an intangible form of combination such as price leadership, there is little room left for the exercise of one's judgment. The smaller business men must charge a price which they have had no voice in fixing; and the only choice left to the consuming public is that of choosing the particular spot at which to pay out its money. This is the outstanding fact in the testimony of Mr. Randall cited above which was brought out by the questioning by Mr. Arnold and the chairman of the Temporary National Economic Committee. The restricted area in which independent judgment may be exercised is that factor which is at the same time the symptom of monopoly and unifies basically all forms of monopoly.

The elimination of the opportunity for exercising one's own judgment which is the consequence of the development of monopoly, reproduces in our national economy the conditions which in a totalitarian regime, through the operation of a one-party system and a single slate of candidates for office, prevent the electorate from using their judgment in the political field.

Price leadership and its corollaries such as "live-and-let-live" policies create an effective mirage to hide the use of monopolistic tactics. For one thing, there is the continuing presence of a number of business entities, which makes it appear that the free enterprise system is being observed. Considering the monopoly problem from this point of view, it is no exaggeration to state that the control by a limited number of concerns is one of the most important and difficult antitrust problems which we have to face. On the one hand, monopoly is difficult to prove where 80 or 90 per cent of an industry is controlled by a few companies. On the other hand, except for exceptional instances such as obtain in the automobile industry, the general trend as shown by the investigations of the Temporary National Economic Committee is not to compete on price. And even in the automobile industry competition operates only within certain limits.

The Basing Point System as a Form of Price Leadership

In the summer of 1948 a decision of the United States Supreme Court outlawed a highly perfected form of price leadership known as the basing or multiple point system, which operated in a large number of important industries. An analysis of the effects of this decision in the light of the method of operation of the basing point system should be of value in determining the general role played by monopoly implementation in furthering concentration of economic power.

According to the Federal Trade Commission, "A remarkably large number of industries have resorted to this type of price control, including those producing iron and steel, pig iron, cement, lime, lumber and lumber products, brick, asphalt shingles and roofing, window glass, white lead, metal lath, building tile, floor tile, gypsum plaster, bolts, nuts and rivets, cast iron soil pipe, range boilers, valves and fittings, sewer pipes, paper and paper products, salt, sugar, corn derivatives, industrial alcohol, linseed oil, fertilizers, chemicals, transportation equipment, and power cable." [22]

The essence of the basing point system is price uniformity on a delivered price basis, regardless of the point of delivery or the point of origin of the products; that is, it involves a refusal to sell at f.o.b. prices. To exemplify the mechanics of this system, let us take the steel industry. For about 20 years prior to 1924, the United States Steel Corporation — and therefore practically all other steel companies — sold steel products at the Pittsburgh base price plus freight to destination. That is to say, no matter where the product originated, the prices quoted were the mill prices at Pittsburgh, plus freight from Pittsburgh. In extreme cases — as, for example, when the fabricating plant using steel products was located on property adjoining a steel mill in the Chicago area — freight was charged from Pittsburgh even though the product could well be tossed over the fence to the consumer.*

The characteristic feature of the manner of operation of the basing point system, is that it works by automatic formula. Each producer knows the price at the buyer's basing point; and, regardless of either the seller's or the buyer's location, quotes a delivered price composed of the basing price plus the specified freight tariff from the basing-point to the customer's location.

What is essential to keep in mind in this connection is that in order for all producers to quote identical prices it is not necessary to get together for conspiratorial purposes. All that is necessary is for each firm to calculate its bids by the same formula. The United States government has, in fact, "received bids so identical that they were carried out to the fourth decimal place." [23]

In commenting upon the above, David Lynch states that, "the fruits of collusion are had without overt forces of collusion." The conspiracy is there, but it is invisible.

Whatever its form and the claims of its beneficiaries, the fact is that the basing point system is an effective device in a new setting to restrain trade and to secure the benefits of oligopoly. Professor F. A. Fetter of Princeton University told the TNEC that "the basing point practice is far and away the most successful single device that large American business . . . has hit upon in the last 75 years." [24] Under this system, "price competition is for all practical purposes obliterated

---

* The quotations given in this chapter are from the hearings before the Temporary National Economic Committee as cited by David Lynch in *The Concentration of Economic Power.*

since all producers charge identical delivered prices regardless of the destination or the place of origin of the commodity. It is a system of reciprocity among oligopolists." [25]

This system was applied to numerous industries for many decades when, in the summer of 1948 the basing point system in the cement industry was outlawed by the Supreme Court. As a result of that decision, other industries, notably steel, began introducing f.o.b. prices plus actual freight charges to points of destination.

The immediate aftermath of the elimination of the basing point system were decreases, largely geographical, in the supplies of certain commodities; increases in prices, suspension of activities in some fields, notably in highway construction, and a general business nervousness and perplexity.

The decision of the Supreme Court was of epochal significance in that it condemned a practice which, through wholesale violations of the principle of free competition, brought about virtual monopoly in important industries but operated in such a manner as to render difficult an identification of its anti-competitive nature.

The Trade Association and Free Enterprise

According to David Lynch, "Many monopolistic methods have been implemented through trade associations, particularly the basing point system and price leadership." [26] Ostensibly their aim is to serve the public good by promoting efficiency. In reality, according to the findings of the Temporary National Economic Committee, these associations have exhibited considerable efficiency in forestalling the free operation of competitive forces, by serving as vehicles of monopoly implementation. As such, they illustrate the contradictory situation into which we, as a nation were led, through the lack of correlation between our preaching and our practice, between our professed philosophy of economics and our business methods. The work of these associations leads business men into the strangely contradictory situation when they act as if their business success depended upon violation of an economic philosophy which they hold in almost the same reverence as their religion.

The ostensible object of the trade associations is bringing industries together to serve the public good by increasing efficiency and reducing costs. "Through them industries may be combined to serve the public interest by increasing efficiency and reducing costs or they may be brought together to conspire against the public and to achieve ends similar to those sought by pools, trusts and other combinations . . . apparently trade associations have been more zealous in supporting

activities which produce the fruits of monopoly than in promoting
methods which reduce production costs, increase efficiency and improve services rendered to the public." [27]

Control of prices, limitation of production, allocation of markets and
restraint of competition among members appear to be a part of the
activities of trade associations as revealed by the TNEC investigations.
Thus, "the Water Valve and Hydrant Group of the Valve and Fittings
Institute combined thirty-one corporations which employed a trade
association to fix and maintain prices." [28]   Examining the ramifications
of the activities of another organization, the Window Glass Manufacturers' Association, the Federal Trade Commission "found that competition had been substantially lessened and that a monopoly in the
sale and distribution of window glass had been effected." [29]

Referring to the activities of another trade association, the Material
Dealers' Alliance, Mr. Lynch says that it "so thoroughly dominated
the area around Pittsburgh and Cleveland that it would require the
most rigorous government regulations to equal it on a comparable scale.
. . . Prices were maintained, output restricted, boycotts threatened,
and the industry rigidly controlled to eliminate almost all types of
competition." [30]

Generally speaking, the methods employed by trade associations
to restrain competition include the following: organization of price
reporting schemes, use of open price systems, development of common
cost-accounting procedures, collection and distribution of statistics,
standardization of accounts, exchange of credit information, agreement upon uniform terms of sale, and the adoption of other uniform
policies with respect to quality, service, and prices.   What relation
these activities have to the vaunted *profession de foi* of serving the
public good through business efficiency can be gathered from the fact
that "between 1928 and 1937 sixty-five important industries were ar-
raigned before the Federal Trade Commission for unlawful restraints
of trade involving trade associations." [31]

As a consequence of the incompatibility between their profession
and their practice — together with the omnipresent nature of their
activities — trade associations' tactics are undermining the economic
values which we consider as inherent in the American tradition to a
greater extent than most of the other present day vehicles of monopoly.
Built upon the foundation of concentrated economic power — the consequence of the earlier monopoly formation through the destruction
of competitors — these newer methods of monopoly implementation
are thwarting effectively the historical efforts of the American people
to control their social environment for the benefit of the nation as a

whole rather than for that of a select few. By tampering with the unobstructed operation of the profit motive these methods are working to the detriment of economic justice and the full development of American democracy.

[1] David Lynch, *The Concentration of Economic Power*, Columbia University Press, pp. 173-174.

[2] *Ibid.*, p. 174.

[3] *Ibid.*, p. 174.

[4] George P. Comer, *"Price Leadership,"* Winter, 1940, issue of *Land and Contemporary Problems*, Duke University Law School, p. 61.

[5] David Lynch, *The Concentration of Economic Power*, p. 174.

[6] George P. Comer, *"Price Leadership,"* Winter, 1940, issue of *Law and Contemporary Problems*, Duke University Law School, p. 62.

[7] *Ibid.*, p. 63.

[8] David Lynch, *The Concentration of Economic Power*, p. 175, Columbia University Press.

[9] *Ibid.*, p. 175.

[10] Quoted from Hearings before the Temporary National Economic Committee, Part 27, p. 14250.

[11] Quoted from Hearings before the Temporary National Economic Committee, Part 19, p. 10592.

[12] Quoted fom Hearings before the Temporary National Economic Committee, Part 27, p. 14282.

[13] Quoted from Hearings before the Temporary National Economic Committee, Part 27, p. 14282.

[14] Quoted from Hearings before the Temporary National Economic Committee, Part 27, p. 2099.

[15] Quoted from Hearings before the Temporary National Economic Committee, Part 16, p. 9045.

[16] Quoted from Hearings before the Temporary National Economic Committee, Part 16, p. 9040.

[17] Quoted from Hearings before the Temporary National Economic Committee, Part 5, p. 2088.

[18] Quoted from Hearings before the Temporary National Economic Committee, Part 5, pp. 2086-2087.

[19] Quoted from Hearings before the Temporary National Economic Committee, Part 5, p. 2089.

[20] David Lynch, *The Concentration of Economic Power*, p. 182, Columbia University Press.

[21] Quoted from Hearings before the Temporary National Economic Committee, Part 5, p. 2090. Italics supplied.

[22] Quoted from Hearings before the Temporary National Economic Committee, Part 5, p. 1897.

[*] After protracted proceedings by the Federal Trade Commission the steel industry abandoned the Pittsburgh plus plan and adopted the multiple basing point system with arbitrary differentials among many of the base prices, such as $3.00 per ton over Pittsburgh at Birmingham and $1.50 at Chicago.

[23] Quoted from Hearings before the Temporary National Economic Committee, Part 5, p. 1897.

[24] Quoted from Hearings before the Temporary National Economic Committee, Part 5, p. 1939.

[25] *Ibid.*

[26] David Lynch, *The Concentration of Economic Power*, p. 212, Columbia University Press.

[27] *Ibid.*, p. 212.

[28] Quoted from Hearings before the Temporary National Economic Committee, Part 25, pp. 1741-1742.

[29] Quoted from Hearings before the Temporary National Economic Committee, Part 25, p. 3318.

[30] David Lynch, *The Concentration of Economic Power*, Columbia University Press, p. 213.

[31] David Lynch, *The Concentration of Economic Power*, pp. 212-213.

CHAPTER IX

Social Ideals and Economic Reality

It is one of the ironies of history that concentration of economic power to a high degree has taken place in a country whose people are proud of a system of government intended to be the executor of the national will — understood as the will of the majority. It is perhaps an even greater irony that this concentration has taken place in a country which glories in the tradition of an individualistic philosophy of private enterprise and free competition.

This concentration of economic power, moreover, was brought about in America whose early leaders were already concerned with the problem of monopoly long before conditions had matured which provided a fertile soil for its growth. From the earliest days of this republic, up to the present, the theme of warning against monopoly has hardly varied. Thomas Jefferson, writing from Paris, "protested against the failure to include an explicit provision to outlaw the evil in the federal constitution . . ."[1] As far back as 1811, Gouverneur Morris wrote to Livingston, "The word 'monopoly' is of dangerous efficiency . . . it may turn the current of opinion against you."[2] Years later, on September 6, 1944, President Roosevelt, writing to Secretary of State Hull, stated that "during the past century the United States has developed a tradition in opposition to private monopolies. The Sherman and Clayton Acts have become as much a part of the American way of life as the due process clause of the Constitution."[3]

And yet, as Dr. Edward H. Levi points out, "despite the strong anti-monopoly tradition in this country . . . concentration of economic control in the sense that a few companies together control the major output of an industry is the standard pattern of American business."[4] Monopoly is an accepted fact. Whether it implies partial control, or is designated as "imperfect competition," whether it appears as a duopoly, or an oligopoly, or whether it is hidden under seemingly disunited methods of monopolistic manipulations, the mass of the people feel it in their daily lives. The farmer, the worker, the small business man and the consumer generally come up against monopolistic obstructions in the form of discretionary controls over prices and supplies.

Walton Hamilton considers that managerial discretion is substituted at "many points where the market once controlled" and that entire areas of industrial activity are removed from "the automatic play of supply and demand." [5]   The evolution away from competition has reached such a state of affairs "that," says Hamilton, "in instances in which the activities of huge concerns converge upon a sensitive price structure, a spot market responding to competitive forces has come to be regarded as too dangerous to be employed as an instrument of industrial regulation." [6]   Professor Ben W. Lewis points out that "important economic decisions are not ground out by impersonal competitive exchange in an open and driving market; they are made quite personally, by men — relatively few men — whom we do not choose and over whom we have only the most tenuous controls." [7]

The competitive system, then, which can be considered as fairly characteristic of our economy during the first half of the 19th century, is disintegrating under the impact of a monopolistic onslaught on our economic life implied in the term "managerial discretion." That is competition is giving way to "managerial discretion" over our economy. Considering the extent and the tempo of the development of private economic power in recent years — and that in the last quarter of 1945, mergers and acquisitions reached the highest level since 1931 — it is safe to venture the statement that, at least in our vital industries, competition as a regulator of our economic life is coming to be a memory of the past. While we cling to our anti-monopoly tradition, and seem in a resigned fashion to be apprehensive at the progress of monopoly, we little realize that we are being hurried along by powerful economic currents which are sweeping away the motivation of our economic life. The very fact that there are important areas in our economy in which a spot market responding to competitive forces is regarded as "too dangerous to be employed as an instrument of industrial regulation" reveals the strength of these antisocial forces and conveys a threatening portent of things to come, as far as our free enterprise tradition is concerned.

The problem is to find ways and means of making our system of political democracy serve more efficiently than heretofore our tradition of economic liberalism. That is legislation must be used to reverse the trend towards the totalitarian collectivism of big business. This presupposes a searching and fearless analysis of the factors and forces — legal, economic, psychical and political — which have been undermining our national efforts to realize the ideal of economic opportunity.

In one form or another the intrinsic causes of the great social upheavals of the past can be related to the encroachment of private interests on universal access to economic resources, either in the form of land and other natural factors of production or in the more complex technological refinements of the present day. Their control determines to a large extent the control of the nation's economy.

Despite the obvious and fundamental fact that monopoly involves a narrowing of the area of competitive access to economic resources, this has hardly ever been given its proper weight in the consideration of our economic problems. Such a critical flaw in reasoning appears the more strange since accessibility to these resources is the essence of the world's problems, past and present. It should be considered as the all-important factor in the problems with which we are now being confronted.

If man had no access, direct or indirect, to economic resources, he and the society of which he is a part would perish.

Our antitrust legislation deals with the American manifestations of this momentous factor around which revolves the present day universal struggle between antipodal economic theories. But it is more than probable that the very universality of this question is responsible for the comparatively slight attention that has been devoted to the enforcement of antitrust legislation. The less general economic problems are more perceptible and easier to grasp than fundamental problems and lend themselves more readily to popular consideration. But a successful approach to the problem of accessibility to our economic resources — understood as competitive accessibility — is associated with the consideration of antitrust activities as being of crucial significance to the preservation of the American tradition.

In considering competitive accessibility to economic resources as barred by monopoly, we as a democratic nation are confronted with a problem that goes to the root of the question of whether we are masters of our own destiny or playthings in the hands of fate — whether we are to control our social environment or whether the environment is to control us. The idea implicit in our governmental organization is to give us the means to control our environment in accordance with the dictates of reason enlightened by our national ideals. The activities of the Congress of the United States, of the state legislatures and of the courts are theoretically directed to that end. The very process of lawmaking as it involves committee hearings and debates in the legislative bodies suggests that what is sought is to make laws the expression of a reasoned attitude towards the problems with which lawmakers are confronted, whatever fault may be found with the reasoning itself. There is usually the attempt to base discussions on facts, to correlate the facts and to establish causal sequences between them, even if these attempts quite frequently suffer from bias, lack of understanding, outside pressure and absence of objectivity. The implicit idea in law-making and in court decisions is to place the law of causality under conditions in which it can operate to bring about social and economic relationships reflecting our national ideals. As concerned with accessibility to economic resources, the task of legislation in our capitalistic democracy implies the obligations to have the privately owned resources used in the best interests of all.

The several varieties of our anti-monopoly legislation, notably the Sherman Antitrust and the Federal Trade Commission Acts, give expression to the idea of this obligation in two forms. One concerns the direct access to economic resources; the other, the indirect access — through the consideration of the relation between prices and trade practices. So far as direct access is concerned, the theory is to prevent the monopolization of economic resources. With respect to indirect access the aim is to eliminate the unfair trade practices, since these interfere with free competition and are reflected in prices which bar competitive access to economic resources.

Democracy operates through legislation as expressive of the will of the people. Since antitrust legislation is the only legislative weapon we have which deals in a fundamental way with the question of a democratic utilization of our economic resources, it is the embodiment of the American concept of economic freedom. Its success means the fulfillment of our historical ideals; its failure augurs protracted economic crises, an increasing sharpening of economic maladjustmens and an accompanying social fermentation. The resulting chaos may mold our psychology into a fatalistic acceptance of a social and economic order which is the negation of our traditional values. The only alternative to antitrust prosecutions in our democracy is a planned economy which, however, may lead to economic dictatorship.

The Fatalistic Trend in Our History.

As we have seen, monopoly, unfair trade practices, and the present day inconspicuous methods of monopoly implementation are undermining our tradition of individual economic freedom. They obstruct the progress of our efforts to control our social environment through the application of the American democratic principle of a conscious and reasoned influence on the course of economic life. But unlike the inimical forces with which we had to contend in the days of the conquest of the frontier, the anticompetitive forces elude efforts at effective control. The same thing can be said of antisocial forces in general. They elude control because of the difficulty of identifying the laws of causal sequences involved in the action of social forces, and the still greater difficulty of acting in accordance with whatever knowledge of these laws has been gained through historical experience. This accounts for the fact that momentous historical changes have so often been brought about through revolutions. Revolutions represent the consummation of the drive of fatalistic forces, as contrasted with evolutionary social mutations. The latter would follow as a result of conscious control of the social environment, guided by a social ideal and not by the interests of an individual or a group in power.

Fatalism, as applied to the history of human society, implies the idea that social changes are determined inevitably, irrespective of the social will. A conspicuous example of the role of fatalism in the social history of mankind is that associated with the Marxian theory. According to Marx, "the result of development — the new in history — is prepared by the entire march of the old, of the previous stages, and the new comes to replace the old in accordance with an inner, immanent requirement."[8]

The development of concentrated economic power in America — the traditional land of free enterprise — against the will of the American people as manifested in legislation and political and other collective expressions of views, indicates the action of a fatalistic force which has had a determining influence on our economic history. The consciousness of the inexorable drive of this force is revealed in the warnings of the intellectually advanced elements of the population. It is given expression in official reports of governmental agencies; for example, the Antitrust Division of the U. S. Department of Justice, which speaks of the "inevitable"[9] economic forces which have brought about a high degree of monopolization in this country. It is implied in the statement of the Federal Trade Commission in its report to Congress that "unless some action is taken to curb the power of giant corporations the country will go 'down the road to collectivism.'"[10]

Whatever the future holds for the industrial countries of Western Europe—whether the drive of inevitable forces will be consummated in a social revolution, or whether it will be counteracted by economic injections of the Marshall Plan type — the feeling seems to be growing that the struggle for economic freedom in this country is not lost. It is manifesting itself in the greater attention paid to our antitrust activities; and in the increasing public, as well as official, interest in the problem of monopoly, as shown by comprehensive Congressional investigations into various phases of the concentration of economic power.

Thus, the need for democratic liberation of our economy from the fetters of monopoly is being increasingly felt as the developments in the outside world become threatening. The onward march of communism in Eastern Europe and Asia, the rise of socialism in Great Britain and the thoughts of nationalization of basic industries in the continental Western European countries, are manifestations of trends towards radically new forms of economic organization. Added to this is the growing doubt that the Marshall Plan will solve the fundamental problems of the countries to which it is applied. And still further, there is the failure to settle the fate of Germany, a country which occupies a strategic position in the economy of Europe.

Despite the false appearances resulting from artificial injections, and although the real facts have become less apparent on the surface than before the inauguration of the Marshall Plan, Western Europe, as well as most of the result of the world, is off its moorings. No historian or economist worth his calling can admit that it could be otherwise, con sidering the radical social and economic dislocations caused by the long years of two destructive world wars and by the Russian communist revolution.

Conflicts of interests between social groups such as are generated by deep-seated economic and social maladjustments, have always had a profound effect on the course of history. Conflicts of interests between tribe and tribe, between nations and nations, and between groups and groups within nations have played an important part in the development of human society, in that they have affected to a considerable degree the nature of social changes.

Upon the possibility of counteracting in this country the seemingly fatalistic trend towards radically new forms of economic life depends our hopes of keeping within limits conflicts of interests between economic groups here. These conflicts are bound to become acute if the country is not freed from the dictatorship of concentrated economic power. That is, the economic factor may yet get the best of the cultural factors and of traditional ideals and prepare a fertile ground for a violent expression of social discontent. The choice between evolution and revolution lies in the *timely* settlement of social conflicts. In our favor are the peculiarities of the historical evolution of American life and the vitality of its traditional ideals. These, combined with the fact that our country escaped the destructive effects of the second world war, may enable us to meet the basic problem of the competitive utilization of economic resources in an evolutionary rather than a revolutionary way.

Action and Counteraction

Generally speaking, violent clashes of interests have led to a violent solution of social conflicts, at important historical periods in Europe and elsewhere. In America, although we have had some such violent

clashes — mostly of a localized nature — the great social changes have
been made peacefully. This has been made possible by an orderly
process of modifying existing laws and by the development of greater
opportunities for the economically weaker elements of the population.
The one exception is what is often called the Second American Revolution — the war between the States. This conflict revolved around
the Negro slave as private property. The bitter contentions could not
be settled peacefully in a legal manner, because the sense of ownership
was fortified by the feeling of racial superiority and the Southern idea
of the Negro as a working animal or even a thing.

The intensity of social changes which involve a conflict of interests
is interwoven with the relation between action and counteraction.
The more violent the action in the form of oppression or social injustice
in general, the more violent will be the counteraction; that is, the more
probable will be a revolutionary solution of the clash of interests.
The more moderate the action, the more certain is a pragmatic solution
of social controversies.

It was in virtue of this principle that the Marxian forecast of a proletarian revolution was not realized in the industrially developed countries of Europe — the expansion of capitalism combined with colonial
exploitation softened economic oppression. In the 19th century America, the expansion of capitalism was blended with the conquest of a
rich continent, carried on through the individualistic conquest of the
frontier. It led to an even more moderate relation between action and
counteraction than in the Western European democracies which were
still affected to some extent by the legacy of absolutism and feudalism.

Without discounting the strength of the altruistic motive, an important consideration in the current American foreign policy appears
to be anxiety to prevent the present misery and suffering in Western
Europe from expressing itself in violent counteraction against capitalism. The program of aid to Western Europe embodied in the Marshall
Plan contemplates the development and full utilization of the productive capacity of Western Europe. Such development it is hoped,
will prove to be an antidote to the trend towards socialism or communism.

During the depression of the thirties, it was felt that timely measures
taken by the government prevented dissatisfaction with intolerable
conditions in America from developing into violent counteraction.
These measures instituted a system of public works — an old idea
which proved to be of temporary value as far back as the 5th century
B.C. in the Athens of Pericles. Instituting public works, under the
WPA, CWA, CCC, besides being a relief measure, was thought of as

a means to keep the unemployed occupied and to prevent discontent from developing into violence.

There are outstanding and reputable economists who propose the adoption of this expedient as part of a long time economic program, accepting, apparently, as unavoidable the recurrence of acute economic crises.   Whatever the possibility of repeating periodically this experiment in governmental semi-philanthropy, the fact is that it is social escapism and, as such, is bound to have in the long run untoward economic and moral consequences.   Since it does not remove the causes of economic crises, these are bound to recur; and their cumulative effect may lead to an unforeseen catastrophe.   It also makes large sections of labor feel that they do not "belong", that they are not an integral and necessary part of the national economy, in that work has to be invented to keep them alive.   The feeling of being pariahs in a society which is geared to the production of abundance is fertile soil for the development of an intolerant attitude towards the existing social order.

In a nation like ours, the national economy cannot be considered as functioning in accordance with its ideals of free enterprise and free competition if it is necessary to provide, periodically, for mending the social cracks by means of measures like the NRA, or public works — whatever their immediate usefulness.   Since most of these measures involve temporary restrictions of production, price fixing, and other restrictive marketing practices, they are the negation of the basic tenets of the capitalism of free enterprise.   If applied too often, they may prove disastrous to the principle upon which American life is founded.

It is not a question of the inherent worth and value of public works. They can be useful, they have been useful when they filled a real need and when they were properly directed.   It is when the extent of public works becomes so large that they must make up for an almost complete economic paralysis — as happened in the thirties — that they have a demoralizing effect on society; inasmuch as they reveal a breakdown of an economic system which has to resort to artificial injections to keep going.

The artificial measures that had to be injected into our economy to keep discontent from assuming an acute form, and the advocacy of such measures as a permanent program for expected future dislocations, point to the fact that political democracy alone cannot keep a proper balance between action and counteraction.   It must be fortified by economics.   And the important question is, by what kind of economics — a system designed to keep the social organism alive by periodical hypodermic shots, or economics based on the control of the social environment. The injection procedure implies submission to anti-social forces; it savors of fatalism. The control method is based upon the consciousness of power to regulate economic conditions as a means to preserve the social ideals of democratic people.

Democracy as a Free Agent

Control involves the overcoming of resistance. In the case of the physical environment, control consists of breaking down the resistance of matter and overpowering the action of physical forces. In the case of the social environment, control is concerned with the resistance of established social relationships and the challenge of antisocial forces. In a capitalist democracy, the social good is supposed to be fulfilled through the working of free competition. Anything that obstructs competition, then, is considered, in public opinion and in legislation, as a force detrimental to the public good — as an antisocial force. The effectiveness of the power of the antisocial forces which interfere with competition and undermine the institution of free enterprise, is the measure of the weakness of the collective free will as expressive of the majority of the population.

Antisocial tendencies are generated by economic maladjustments. When they are not checked, they override our hopes and aspirations as a free and democratic nation. In a different guise, these forces play the same role, in democracies, as oppression has played in those countries which have overturned their social organization through revolutionary outbreaks. But whereas oppression in such countries was a concentrated and readily recognized phenomenon, antisocial tendencies in a democracy are diffused and ofttimes nebulous.

Antisocial tendencies are the carriers in a democracy of the fatalistic forces of history. Under absolutist dictatorial governments revolutions are the bursting point of the driving pressure of inexorable historical forces. The collective will of a people under oppression reveals itself only at the moment when the social structure is ready to crumble under the three-fold pressure of misery, social injustice and outraged human dignity. It cannot be called free will, for it has no choice. It is driven to counteraction in a violent and elemental outburst. In democracies, on the other hand, antisocial tendencies are supposed to be checked by social action through the means provided by democratic processes of legislation.

In an ideal democratic society, then, the continuous application of legislation — enacted by public bodies elected by the people — gives an outlet to a supposedly reasoned expression of the collective will.

This is the distinctive characteristic of democracies; it is what makes democratic peoples feel that they are masters of their own destiny and not playthings in the hands of blind social forces.

The attitude of democracy towards historical necessity differs from both utopianism and Marxism. Unlike the utopian concept, democracy considers that social changes cannot be brought about at will without regard to time, place, and previous conditions of historical development. It considers that they must be consonant with circumstances of the dynamic operation of the law of causality. The very process of law-making in a democracy, particularly in America, with its emphasis on "checks and balances" and other safeguards against attempts to break historical continuity, is indicative of the belief that social changes must be timely and must be conditioned by facts of life. Again, unlike Marxism, democracy does not hold to the concept of irrepressible economic forces driving humanity towards a socialist state through the two stages of a social revolution and a proletarian dictatorship. Instead, democracy considers that the will of the people can resist the drive of blind forces and that it can do this through the democratic enactment of legislative acts and measures consistent with democratic objectives. That is, in a democracy which is supposed to be the outcome of study, clash of ideas, and widespread publicity designed to obtain the view of the public, the law of causality is brought under control.

In its search for the most effective method of social control, there are, generally speaking, two philosophies with which modern society is confronted: the communist-socialist philosophy and the philosophy of the capitalism of free enterprise. Communism and socialism imply the nationalization of the means of production and distribution, although central planning of economic activities is carried on more intensively as well as in a more rigorous manner under communism than is contemplated under socialism. But since the philosophy of the capitalism of free enterprise envisages competition as the regulator of economic relationships, it is inimical to any centralization of economic activities whether private or governmental. Nevertheless, it is under the banner of free enterprise that the capitalism of monopolies and cartels, symbolizing private centralization, is now fighting for supremacy over communism and socialism as expressive of governmental centralization in the great contest that is taking place in the world today.

Almost as a side issue to this global contest, the genuine capitalism of free enterprise is struggling against tremendous odds to regain the ground which it has lost to monopoly capitalism. Despite the modest position to which it has been relegated it is the capitalism of free enterprise that is most truly representative of the historical American ideal of democracy — as against the collectivist aspirations of communism on the one hand, and fascism as the political expression of monopoly capitalism on the other hand.

That free competition would be hampered in its role of economic regulator was, more than fifty years ago, consciously or unconsciously recognized by the legislative representatives of the American people when they enacted the Sherman Antitrust Act. This recognition was again evident when they had the Sherman Act followed in later years by similar legislative measures, all designed to clear the way for the unobstructed working of free competition. That these measures, however, have not attained the goal envisaged by this legislation is shown by the growth of monopolies and monopolistic combinations, which are centralizing our economic activities and decreasing opportunities for self-employment as well as narrowing the field within which individual initiative can still be exercised. But even though antitrust measures have not been able to totally fulfill their mission, they have retained the seeds of great vitality. This is demonstrated by the fact that despite inimical forces in various forms — such as pressures, insufficient funds, the delays and complexities of court action and hostility in private and official quarters — our antitrust agencies have kept our economy from being completely monopolized, and have reestablished competitive conditions in a number of instances which have come to their attention.

So far as the past is concerned we know that the peaceful method of settlement of conflicts of interest was due to our characteristic type of democracy combined with the fact that it has operated in a distinctive historical period in which the expansion of capitalism has been interwoven with the conquest and settlement of a great continent. We cannot say definitely whether with the coming of normal times we are due for an economic expansion or an economic contraction. But in our attempt to look into the future, we can rely to some extent upon Karl Marx. Despite the fact that Marx was in error in calculating the *consequences* of certain economic trends as reflected in the tempo and intensity of social protest and opposition, his forecast of these trends themselves is generally working out—notably with reference to his theory of the contradictions inherent in capitalism and of the process of concentration of economic power.

According to Marx, production under capitalism, becomes, at a given stage, hampered by what he designates as the contradictions of capitalism, which cause capitalism to contract, and reduce production. Confronted with market uncertainties — which result largely from uncoordinated over-all production and from lack of mass purchasing power — those industries that are in a position of control adopt a policy of restricted production in order to dominate the markets and to safeguard profits. A contradictory situation develops which, in its extreme form, can be characterized as poverty in the midst of plenty — the possibility to produce abundantly and lack of purchasing power to absorb what is or could be produced. Although we hesitate to agree with this theory, the distressing fact is that the area of private control, which makes possible a policy of restricting production, has grown recently in this country to an alarming extent.

That we have entered the period of the contraction of capitalism has been evident for some time. The criterion by which the question of contraction or expansion should be determined relates to the consideration of a smooth and uninterrupted flow of economic life combined with the economic comfort and security of the population. Whatever statistics can be brought forth to show a great increase in production in this or that industry or in industry as a whole, the fact of an economic crisis is an index of contraction of a given economic system. Production is a relative concept; it has no significance if it is considered outside of its relation to the welfare of the various groups of the population. The unprecedented economic crisis of the thirties was the first potent sign that capitalism was contracting. It interrupted to a distressing degree the flow of economic life and necessitated heroic and many economically unsound measures to bring about a normal economic life for a few years, or rather a semblance of a normal life. for, as was noted above there was considerable distress among a considerable segment of the population — in 1939 "eight million families in the United States faced starvation on incomes of less than $750 a year, and another eleven million families fought poverty on incomes between $750 and $1,500." There was developing what was officially designated as a "recession" but which was generally regarded as an oncoming depression which was forestalled by the second World War. Since then the economic picture was blurred by the war, the shadow of the cold war, the war in Korea and the threat of another World War with their enhanced demands on the economy of the country.

Marxism, as was noted, considers that the contradictions of capitalism lead it unavoidably to economic contraction. It is difficult to gloss over the fact that the development of monopoly does lead to economic contraction inasmuch as production is subordinated to considerations of market domination. The statements of Congressman Celler and Walter Reuther, quoted earlier with regard to steel shortages, point to the nature of the contraction of capitalism. The problem before us, at this crucial moment of world's history, is to disprove the Marxian contention by a successful return to a competitive economy. That sooner or later we will face an acute situation is also reasonable to expect, in view of the world revolt against the domination of private interests and against an ever-growing monopolistic control of the resources which form the foundation of life. That in another possible economic crisis we can expect more desperate protests on the part of the masses can also be assumed. As Professor Clair Wilcox points out: "Monopoly impairs democracy's ability to defend itself in time of war. National defense requires an expansion of output; monopoly seeks to augment its profit by restricting output and maintaining price. It thus obstructs the procurement of arms and supplies, increases the cost of defense, adds to the burden of debt and taxation, and undermines national morale . . . Monopoly threatens democracy, too, when its contribution to industrial paralysis, to unemployment and to distributive inequality, induces those widespread attitudes of hopelessness and resentment that make ready converts for the propagandists of revolutionary change." [11] In the words of the Federal Trade Commission: "The capitalist system of free initiative is not immortal, but is capable of dying and of dragging down with it the system of democratic government. Monopoly constitutes the death of capitalism and the genesis of authoritarian government." [12]

The implication of this statement is clear and definite. It is a repetition in a different form of this Commission's statement, quoted earlier and of statements by the Antitrust Division of the United States Department of Justice as well as by public spirited citizens generally. It finds an echo in the views of the masses who appear to take a defeatist attitude with respect to the possibility of undermining the concentrated economic power. In all these views and statements there is a definite premonition that if the trend towards the monopolization of economic resources is not controlled so as to open the way to individual economic freedom, our economic system is doomed.

The fact that this trend has reached a point at which it appears alarming, shows its fatalistic nature. We are called to control it at time when it has acquired such momentum in other countries that it is threatening to engulf the world, and is threatening to deprive us of our legacy of economic freedom and our cultural heritage.

Shall we, then, allow this trend to continue unchecked by law and resign ourselves to a fatalistic acceptance of it? It it had not been for the fact that we succeeded in subjugating the inimical forces of nature, through the control of the law of causality, we would still be at the mercy of these forces with all that it implies in suffering, privation and disease. But in the physical world fatalism became a myth when adequate means were found to apply the knowledge gained from analyzing the operation of the law of causal sequences. Fatalism could become a myth in the world of social relationships also, if laws of causal sequences in social phenomena could be ascertained and controlled as they are in the world of nature.

A valuable laboratory for a study and analysis of the forces which obstruct our efforts to control these laws is the problem of monopoly. In it are concentrated the difficulties associated with a possibility of a reasoned and effective social action.

[1] Edward H. Levi, "The Antitrust Laws and Monopoly," *The University of Chicago Law Review*, February, 1947, p. 156.

[2] *Ibid.*, p. 153.

[3] *Ibid.*, p. 156.

[4] *Ibid.*, p. 153.

[5] Walton Hamilton, *Antitrust in Action*, Investigation of Concentration of Economic Power, Temporary National Economic Cmmittee, Monograph No. 16, p. 13.

[6] *Ibid.*, p. 13.

[7] Ben. W. Lewis, "Antitrust laws: A Symposium," *American Economic Review*, June, 1949, p. 705.

[8] Alexandrov, *et. al.* The History of Philosophy, (Moscow, 1940) Vol. III, p. 277.

[9] *United States versus Economic Concentration and Monopoly*, report to the Monopoly Subcommittee of the Committee on Small Business, House of Representatives, p. 34.

[10] *Report of the Federal Trade Commission on the Merger Movement*, Washington, 1948, p. 69.

[11] Clair Wilcox, *Competition and Monopoly in American Industry*, Temporary National Economic Committee, Monograph No. 21, p. 18.

[12] Report of the Federal Trade Commission on the Merger Movement, Washington, D. C., p. 69.

CHAPTER X

Difficulty of Appraising the Nature of Monopoly

In the American ideology the forces which hinder competitive access to economic resources are antisocial forces. They are destructive of our social ideals of freedom and opportunity. The origin of the fatalistic pressure of these forces on our economy is to be found in the lag of time between the appearance of conditions which give rise to monopoly, and the historical moment when the impact of the monopoly-generating force is felt and recognized. It is within this period that the basic antisocial force from which all the others originate, the misuse of the profit motive, finds a wide and unhampered field of action.

Human relationships change. The change usually takes place slowly, or in such a manner as not to be clearly seen at the time the changes are occurring. With the passage of time the changed relationships solidify, and it is only then that their effect and significance become apparent. When the Sherman Antitrust Law was enacted, an earnest prosecution of the nascent monopolies would have encountered less resistance than it does now, when monopolies rest their power on a considerably greater centralization of industry with a correspondingly stronger influence on public affairs.

The economic development of America presents a vivid instance of environmental influences which, working through the element of time, retarded the full realization by the public of the growing concentration of economic power as a factor destructive of the American way of life.

The tempo and sweep of the conquest and settlement of the American continent, the wealth in natural resources, and the expanse of the country were such that even after the frontier was reached and periodical depressions revealed basic economic maladjustments, only sporadically was attention paid to the antisocial forces which began to make themselves felt in the form of monopolies.

That is, the dynamics of the settlement and the expansion of America, combined with the fact that sufficient elbow room was left for a long time after economic opportunities began to contract with the disappearance of the frontier, kept people's minds off these forces. Concentrated economic power therefore succeeded, in a space of a few decades, in dominating the American economy. It was only when the depression of the 30's revealed the basic significance of our economic maladjustments that we became conscious, although not yet fully, of a serious threat to our traditional concept of economic freedom.

Ironically enough, the first great merger movement occurred shortly after the passage of the Sherman Antitrust Act, between 1898 and 1903. "That period saw the beginning of International Silver, International Paper, American Linseed, United Shoe Machinery, Standard Sanitary, American Snuff, International Salt, American Can, Eastman Kodak, International Harvester, Corn Products, International Nickel, and E. I. du Pont de Nemours Power Company. It saw the formation of the United State Steel Corporation."[1] By means both fair and foul, through legitimate procedure as well as through dishonest and disreputable tactics, centralized control of industry was increasing in scope and intensity partly through mergers and consolidations of producing units, but as time went on, mostly through financial combinations of the investment banking type. The advantages of mass production were nullified by the use of power inherent in the concentrated private control of economic resources to subordinate public welfare to considerations of private interest.

Varying Legal Interpretations of the Nature of Monopoly

The onslaught of the forces of concentrated economic power as they have forced their way through in the peculiar conditions of the American environment, have bred confusion in our attitude towards monopoly and monopolistic practices. This confusion shows itself in the fluctuating opinions of the courts with regard to the nature of monopolistic combinations. These opinions, of course, have a direct significance in the study of the problem of monopoly. In addition, they present us with an unusual opportunity to observe the intricacies involved in identifying the dynamics of the causal sequences which determine economic phenomena.

The period of the roaring twenties which followed the first World War, during which period an unusual number of mergers and consolidations took place, offers fruitful material for such study, if attention is centered on the contrast between the principles implied in the court decisions of that period and those adopted by some courts in later years. The period was characterized by a hilarious optimism. America was in the midst of apparently limitless prosperity, and the contrast with Europe was so strong as to breed in us the confidence that no serious depression could occur in the United States.

In this atmosphere of optimism, well-being, full employment, little attention was paid to the problem of monopoly. No apprehension was felt concerning the fact that, at this particular time, the second great merger movement was taking place since the passage of the Sherman Antitrust Act, in the course of which "more than 1,238 consolidations of business firms took place, resulting from the disappearance of approximately 7,000 companies." [2]   If anything, the movement toward mergers was considered as another sign of progress; and it was actually hailed as the beginning of an economic millenium. "The numerous mergers and combinations, the newly developed chain stores, and similar business consolidations, were considered as so many evidences of a new-found economic advantage identified with mass purchasing, mass selling, and mass manufacturing." [3]

Two outstanding jurists, Robert Marx and Schmidt proclaimed that "the day of the blatant trust-buster is definitely over"; and that "mergers, combines and perhaps even monopolies are permitted and welcomed." [4]

That the situation had been misjudged became evident when "the new economic advantage of mass purchasing, mass selling, and mass manufacture" made possible by mergers failed to materialize. It became even more evident when the country — instead of reaping the benefits of "the new economic freedom" — was plunged into the worst depression of its history.

The estimate of the causal relations between the phenomena of mass manufacture, mass purchasing, and mass selling, on the one hand, and permanent prosperity on the other, had proved to be incorrect. But until the depression revealed the true relation between the various factors in our economic organization, and was shown to have been largely the result of insufficient purchasing power, little attempt was made to see in their real light the causal relations between mass manufacture and mass purchasing as they were ultimately reflected in mass selling.

Those who hailed mergers and combinations as presaging a new economic freedom, and were benevolently inclined towards monopolies, overlooked certain facts. These facts were brought out years later in the course of the Temporary National Economic Committee investigation which reported that monopoly in general is not conducive to economic progress, "that the monopolist may be reluctant to make use of inventions if they would compel him to scrap existing equipment or if he believes that their ultimate profitability is in doubt. He may introduce innovations and cut costs, but instead of moving goods by price reduction he is prone to spend large sums on alternative methods of promoting sales; his refusal to cut prices deprives the community of any gain. The monopolist may voluntarily improve the quality of his product and reduce its price, but no threat of competition compels him to do so." [5]

There is no doubt that if a constant balance could have been maintained between mass production, mass buying, and mass selling, our economy would have been functioning without any dislocations. The very fact, however, that there were dislocations and that they were serious enough to lead to an economic crisis, shows that something had happened that upset the balance — with dire consequences to the national economy, and with little credit to our ability to identify causal relations as a working basis for a program of action. Mass production was not matched by mass selling; surpluses appeared; and business crashed.

Despite full employment — in 1929 there were only 429,000 unemployed [6] — there was a barrier between the mass of the population and the economic resources of the country. It was the artificial rigidity of prices. "When the depression came it was recognized that price rigidity, *the mark of monopoly or effective trade restrictions*, had played its part." [7] Furthermore, "during the depression, rigid price behavior made readjustment and recovery difficult." Price rigidity had a negative influence on purchasing power. Insufficient buying ability to absorb what was produced was recognized as the basic cause of the depression.

The attitude towards industrial centralization as a favorable factor in economic progress found an echo in the court decisions of the time. The Supreme Court gave United States Steel its sanction as a form of corporation. The concept of size *per se* as a dangerous factor in the power of monopoly was rejected. Size in itself was not considered an offense.

In monopoly cases the courts, until recently, were primarily concerned with abuses rather than with size and the power that is inherent in it. "In 1920, the Supreme Court held that the United States Steel Corporation was not a monopoly because it was not at the time guilty of predatory practices toward competitors." [8] The court stated that, "the law does not make mere size an offense, or the existence of unexerted power an offense." [9] It "referred to the absence of 'unworthy motives' and said that the law requires 'overt acts' as a necessary ingredient of offense." [10]

There are several perplexing angles to the history of court decisions illustrating the peculiarities of interpretation of monopolistic phenomena. While the Supreme Court did not at the time (1920) consider size *per se* as a factor aiding in a monopolistic domination of the market; while it did not object to size in the steel case (1920); and "later, in the International Harvester case (1927), it even found a 64 per cent market control unobjectionable," [11] it frowned upon many of the collusive activities of competing business units on the ground that they were illegal restraints of trade. Thus, under Section 1 of the Sherman Act, the designation of unreasonable restraints of trade was applied to competitors who collectively occupy a small place in the national economy. On the other hand, the undesirability of a concentrated market control vested in a consolidated concern was apparently rejected.

This gave rise to a disconcerting situation which is illustrated by the famous Addyston Pipe and Steel Company case. "That case, decided in 1899, held illegal a conspiracy between six corporations to enhance prices by eliminating competitive bidding in the sale of cast iron pipe." [12] The Department of Justice filed a civil suit in New Jersey against the United States Pipe and Foundry Company and four other companies, alleging both restraint of trade and monopoly. According to the allegations of the Department, "there was effected in 1898 a consolidation of four of the companies who were defendants in the Addyston case. The consolidated company was known as American Pipe and Foundry Company." [13] Later the United States Pipe and Foundry Company was incorporated in New Jersey. This company then acquired the American Pipe and Foundry Company, also the two remaining defendants involved in the Addyston case, as well as a number of other companies. "The government alleges that the United States Pipe and Foundry Company is now the largest manufacturer and distributor of cast iron in the United States." [14]

Thus, the defendants in the original Addystone case, who had been enjoined in 1899 from carrying out their price-fixing conspiracy, were found to have merged into one single company which was now the largest concern in the industry. By merging they had completely eliminated competition among themselves and were not brought to account for several decades, during which the courts ignored the factor of size in the problem of monopoly.

The view that there is no causal relation between size *per se* and the power of monopoly was held by the courts until 1943. Then, after a long time lag, the courts awoke to the consequences resulting from their inconsistency in condemning the lesser evil while approving the greater, and began to relate the power of monopoly to size. This recognition of the law of causality as a dynamic force was presented in a series of notable decisions. The essence of these decisions lies in the shifting away from the view that only abuses are bad in the eyes of the law, toward the belief that the Sherman Act forbids monopolization as such.

Although this change of views was implicit in the District Court's decision in the Pullman case (1945) it was the opinion of Judge Learned Hand in the Alcoa (Aluminum Company of America) case (1943) that first stated the interpretation of the scope of monopoly prohibition which has now been adopted by the Supreme Court. "In the Alcoa case the three senior judges of the Circuit Court of Appeals for the second Circuit Court held that Alcoa had a monopoly of the domestic ingot market, within the meaning of the Sherman Act, even though the company was not found to be guilty of abuses."[15]

In the Alcoa case the courts thought that, irrespective of whether or not there were abuses, the mere existence of great power resulted in price-fixing by Alcoa for the whole market. "When Alcoa sold its products, the mere existence of the power to fix prices, inherent in the monopoly position, could not be distinguished from the exercise of such power. Any distinction between the existence of monopoly power and its exercise was "purely formal".[16] When the monopoly entered the market "the power and its exercise must coalesce". "This," says Wendell Berge, "comes near to holding that size itself is an offense."[17]

This decision marks a turning point in the judicial understanding of the law of causality as it relates to the problem of monopoly. In the earlier decisions, judicial attention had been centered on the static aspects of cases, on the question of actual overt acts or violations of law. In the later decisions, beginning with the Alcoa case, the courts began to consider the potentiality for abuses which was inherent in size. They adopted the dynamic point of view and began to consider the cumulative effects of mergers and consolidations.

An analysis of the difference between the earlier and the later court decisions brings out a factor which is of considerable significance to the study of the problem of monopoly as a phase of the study of social relationships. The later court decisions constitute a decided advance over the earlier decisions in the direction of the solution of the monopoly problem. They represent a more penetrating insight into the relationships that center around the question of free competition versus monopoly power. They exhibit an appreciation of the complexities involved in adequately evaluating causal sequences as these determine the pattern of social relationships. Above all, they show the sense of the dynamic as contrasted with the static concept of the former decisions. It is not so much the actual fact of a given set of relationships as the movement, the potentiality of a given situation that should concern those who deal with social phenomena in whatever capacity they may be — as students, statesmen or jurists.

In the earlier court decisions the legal mind had been in pursuit of the obvious. The courts were interested in what had happened at a given moment, in the palpable violation of the law as exemplified in direct collusive practices. When two independent concerns engaged in collusion to fix prices it was obvious that an open violation of the law occurred. But when these same concerns — as happened in the Addyston case—later merged and then as one concern establisheda price, the courts held at first that there was no violation of the law. The act of collusion was not visible. Yet, the inflexible price, the consequence of the absence of competition, results from both the overt act of collusion and from the act of collusion which is hidden under the merger of two or more concerns. From the point of view of the effects, violations occurred in both cases; but the courts did not seem to realize it until they had shifted their attention from the static to the dynamic poin of view regarding unfair practices.

"The Supreme Court expressly approved the Alcoa decision in the American Tobacco case decided in 1946. In that case the three leading tobacco companies and others were fond guilty in a criminal case of both restraints on trade and of monopoly. The trial judge's instruction permitted a verdict of guilty of monopolization on a finding of power and intent to exclude competitors, even though no actual exclusion was found to have occurred. The conviction was affirmed by the Supreme Court in an opinion holding that actual exclusion of competitors is not necessary to the crime of monopolization." [18] In this connection it should be noted that whereas the court in the United States Steel case had held that "the existence of unexerted power" was not an offense, the court in the Tobacco case held that it was an offense.

With reference to the question of "intent," the judges in the Alcoa case also held to the concept of dynamics in causal relations. They disregarded the formal concept of "specific" intent and considered it obviously in its relation to the potentiality of monopoly power as can be seen from the following excerpt from this decision: "To read the passage as demanding any 'specific' intent, makes nonsense of it, for no monopolist monopolizes unconscious of what he is doing. So here 'Alcoa' meant to keep, and did keep, that complete and exclusive hold upon the ingot market with which it started. That was to 'monopolize' the market, however innocently it otherwise proceeded." [19]

From the point of view of social control as reflected in the conditions governing accessibility to economic resources, these fluctuating opinions of the courts, placing size in its relation to monopoly power, lead to the consideration of the crucial factor in the question of man's influence on his environment. This is the extent to which the knowledge of the right thing to do determines social action — which is essentially a question of proper timing and an understanding of causal sequences. Not only must we know what to do, but we must do it at the right time, at the proper historical moment.

The difficulties presented by the problem of social control lie in the lag of time between the acquisition of knowledge and action based on this knowledge. It is also within this sphere that conditions are generated that determine whether there is to be an evolutionary or a revolutionary solution of a social problem.

Considered from this angle there is room for thought concerning the fact that the courts arrived at the formulation of the monopoly problem in terms of size at a time when the concentration of economic power had attained such a magnitude that the task of enforcing the Sherman Antitrust Act loomed already as a formidable problem. While the process of the concentration of economic power had been taking place all these years, the legal, judicial and to a large extent the economic thinking had been unimpressed by the popular concept of the relation between size and economic abuses. But this concept, under the designation "Big Business," became the battle cry of the farmers' movements whose influence was largely responsible for the enactment of the Sherman Antitrust Act. The idea of bigness and the definite meaning which was attached to it as a source of private economic power, lingered in the popular mind. Whatever the personal views and doubts of politicians, the danger in size — big business — was understood by the rank and file. And their understanding of the danger was embodied in the references to monopolies which were consistently incorporated, election year in, election year out, in the platforms of political parties.

In the view of Justice Douglas "Size . . . should . . . be jealously watched. In the final analysis, size . . . is the measure of the power of a handful of men over our economy. That power can be utilized with lightning speed. It can be benign or it can be dangerous. The philosophy of the Sherman Act is that it should not exist." [20]

The lack of appreciation of the dynamic operation of the law of causality which was responsible for the courts' belated perception of the cumulative effects of the size of monopolistic combinations on the economy of the country, played an important role in the tardiness in recognizing the detrimental effects of concentrated economic power on the preservation of democracy. Of course, the elusive nature of the relationship between economics and democracy, to a large extent, too, delayed this recognition.

Economics and Democracy

The significance of the economic factor as an important determinant of the practice of democracy does not impress itself on the consciousness as readily as do the political ingredients of democracy. To say what you please, to believe what you please, and to vote for whom you please has become an axiom. It does not require a demonstration that when you have these rights you live in a democracy; and that when these rights are abolished or curtailed, you pass into absolutism or totalitarianism. But when waves of unemployment result from depressions it does not occur to the sufferers from these to think of their rights as members of a democratic society.

The reason for the difference in these attitudes lies in the fact that a deprivation of political rights could only be occasioned by the action of a visible force. On the other hand, an economic crisis is the consequence of the action of monopolistic forces whose responsibility in the curtailment of opportunities for capacity production and full employment is seldom, if at all, realized by the majority of the people.

And yet, democracy implies the right of the people to economic opportunities as well as to political equality. Democracy means the power of the people to order their national life in accordance with their ideal of national welfare. In America this ideal is founded on the right of the individual to "life, liberty and the pursuit of happiness." Since the consideration of material well-being cannot be separated from the concept of "pursuit of happiness' nor even from that of liberty, democracy implies economic freedom — the right to economic opportunity as well as to political prerogatives inherent in a representative democratic society.

Despite the ever-increasing progress of the monopolization of economic resources, and despite its visible effects on our economy as revealed in chronic unemployment in times of peace, the significance of economics as an integral part of democracy dawned upon us only when the acute depression of the 30's spread an unprecedented gloom over the nation. This new understanding was also partly due to the popularization, consequent upon developments in the Soviet Union of the Marxian doctrine of economic determinism. The feeling that prevailed at the time, that an unchecked depression can and may result in a revolution, explains largely the ease and rapidity of enactment of the most daring New Deal measures.

It fell to an outstanding American, Justice Douglas of the United States Supreme Court, to formulate with clarity and forcefulness the nature of the relationship between democracy and economics as this relationship is affected by economic maladjustments consequent upon monopolization of access to economic resources. Presented in a dissenting opinion which Justice Douglas wrote in the Columbia Steel case, and which was endorsed by three of his colleagues,[21] it constitutes a landmark in the study of the problem of monopoly.

Justice Douglas' analysis of the relation between industrial power and democracy serves to clarify the role of economics in the practical application of democratic principles. He brings out forcefully the fact that our political prerogatives are being impaired through the curtailment of economic opportunities which is consequent upon the concentration of economic power. His reasoning leads to the formulation of a criterion for the proper evaluation of monopoly and monopolistic practices as deterrents to equitable social and political relationships.

His analysis integrates the economic factor with the political constituents of a valid democracy. "Power that controls the economy," says Mr. Douglas, "should be in the hands of elected representatives of the people, not in the hands of an industrial oligarchy. Industrial power should be decentralized. It should be scattered into many hands so that the fortunes of the people will not be dependent on the whim or caprice, the political prejudices, and the emotional stability of a few self-appointed men."[22]

Further, in the words of Mr. Douglas, the Sherman Antitrust Act "is founded on the theory of hostility to the concentration in private hands of power so great that only a government of the people should have it."[23] It therefore follows that the Sherman Act and other antimonopoly legislation are economic counterparts of the Bill of Rights, which is opposed to the concentration of political power that may become dangerous if all the people do not equally share in it. As a consequence, antitrust legislation should be an object of solicitude to a government founded on the declaration that governments are instituted to guarantee the citizens of a country "life, liberty, and the pursuit of happiness." The implication from Justice Douglas' opinion is that a system of private enterprise working under conditions of free competition is the only system possible, within the framework of a capitalist society, that would guarantee the same rights in the field of economics as the Bill of Rights guarantees in the political field.

In enacting at various times—beginning with the Sherman Antitrust Act—laws dealing with monopoly, monopolistic practices, and restraints of trade, the Congress of the United States has obviously recognized the principle that economic freedom is reflected in freedom of competition and, hence, in the institution of free enterprise. This is shown to be in accordance with our policy of containment of communism. We have assigned to economic freedom — that is, economic opportunity — an appreciable role in a democratic social organization. As against attempts to bolster democracy in some Western European countries by means of economic measures, such as the nationalization of essential economic resources within the framework of capitalism, or the struggle in Eastern Europe to foster a new and allegedly higher type of democracy considered inseparable from a complete collectivization of society, we in this country have held to the doctrine that only private enterprise working under conditions of free competition is capable of sustaining democratic rights and privileges.

The belated appreciation of the relation between democracy and economics, particularly in its anti-monopoly phase, explains to a considerable extent the comparative apathy of the public towards antitrust enforcement in the past. To a certain degree this apathy is traceable to the fact that in this case as well as in economics generally causal sequences are not easily traceable. This leads to considerable perplexity in the formulation of the relations between cause and effect which is a primary condition of rational action in any field.

It is only within the last few years, under the influence of the progress which radical doctrines are making in other parts of the world, that the relation between economic maladjustments and the fulfillment of the American democratic ideal began to impress itself on our minds. It seems that it is life itself, rather than theoretical studies, which is advancing our understanding of the relation between cause and effect in the domain of social relationships.

Under conditions of a strong arm political or economic oppression, the operation of the law of casualty is sufficiently perceptible to make it possible to identify the target upon which to concentrate. On the other hand, when oppression hides under the form of subtle political and economic exploitation, it is difficult to establish the proper causal sequences.

An important aspect of subtle political exploitation is presented by the attempts to minimize the significance of the economic factor in the fulfillment of the aims of democracy or even to divert attention from it by extolling the purely political democratic rights and privileges. The subtlety of economic exploitation notably in the field of monopoly expansion shows itself in a variety of practices, as in the seemingly harmless and apparently innocent use of business methods which, under the guise of fostering efficiency and rational business management, serve the purpose of monopoly implementation. In either case the essential relations between cause and effect as considered in the light of the prerequisites of a full fruition of the democratic ideal are difficult to detect.

In the political field the causal relation between democracy and economics is only beginning to be generally recognized with respect to that phase of economics which concerns the problem of monopoly interference with a competitive access to economic resources. In the economic field, if we take as a representative example the trade associations in their role of a vehicle of subtle monopoly implementation, what is observable is their work in promoting purportedly efficient and uniform business practices. What is not visible to the naked eye is the causal relation between the expansion of monopoly and the promotion of these practices.

The interlacing of these two factors — the lack of perception of the relation between economics and democracy and the elusive character of present day monopoly implementation — is of considerable importance in the consideration of the action of those forces which, as they work through monopoly capitalism, are making mockery of our pretensions at being masters of our destiny by converting our economy into a caricature of private enterprise.

[1] Edward H. Levi, "The Antitrust Laws and Monopoly," *The University of Chicago Law Review*, February, 1947, p. 169.
[2] *Ibid.*, p. 169.
[3] *Ibid.*, p. 170.
[4] *Ibid.*, p. 170.
[5] Clair Wilcox, *Competition and Monopoly in American Industry*, TNEC Monograph, No. 21, pp. 16-17.
[6] *The Economic Almanac* (1941-42), National Industrial Conference Board, p. 123.
[7] Edward H. Levi, *The University of Chicago Law Review*, February, 1947, p. 170. Italics supplied.
[8] Wendell Berge, "The Sherman Antitrust Act and the Enforcement of Competition," *American Economic Review*, May, 1948, p. 173. United States vs. United States Steel Corporation, 251 U. S. 417 (1920).
[9] *Ibid.*, p. 173.
[10] *Ibid.*, p. 173.

[11] *Ibid.*, p. 173. United States vs. International Harvester Company, 274 U. S. 693 (1927).

[12] *Ibid.*, p. 174. Addyston Pipe and Steel Company vs. United States, 175 U. S. 211 (1899).

[13] *Ibid.*, p. 174.

[14] *Ibid.*, p. 174.

[15] *Ibid.*, p. 175.

[16] *Ibid.*, p. 175.

[17] *Ibid.*, p. 175.

[18] *Ibid.*, pp. 175-176.

[19] United States vs. Aluminum Company of America, 148 F2d 416.

[20] United States vs. Columbia Steel Company *et al*, 334 U. S. 495 (1948).

[21] Dissenting opinion of Justice Douglas in United States vs. Columbia Steel Company, *et al.* October term, 1947.

[22] *Ibid.*

[23] *Ibid.*

CHAPTER XI

Monopoly, Government and the Power of Pressure

Governmental action with respect to monopolistic encroachments on individual economic freedom can be properly evaluated when it is considered as a phase of the general problem of the means which are available in a given society to carry out in practice the principles of the social philosophy upon which it is founded. Obviously, these means are the legislative, the executive and the judiciary organs of the government. These are the instruments through which our democracy aims at controlling the social environment.

Social theories, with certain exceptions, generally consider government as essential. Some of the exceptions are found in the communist expectations of a classless society with its withering away of government; in the theory of philosophical anarchism which contends that society can fulfill its duty to its members without government, merely through the unhampered functioning of the supposedly innate altruistic qualities in man; and in the wistful nostalgia of our "rugged individualists." But it is usually felt that composition of a government and the manner in which it is expected to function determine the distinctive nature of a social order and reflect the principles of the social philosophy upon which this order is founded. An absolutist state is distinguished by the concentration of the three governmental powers — legislative, executive and judiciary — in a single institution; while the distinctive mark of a democratic state is the separation of these powers. Although this separation has never been fully carried out, the principles which it reflects have been given sufficient practical validity in democratic countries to be considered as determining the manner in which a democratic social order functions.

The organs of the government are the instrumentalities through which the social philosophy of a nation is carried out. Consequently, in view of the fact that there is such a divergence between the American ideal of free competition and the reality of American economics, the question of the development of monopolies turns logically on the problem of the efficacy of these implements of the national will.

Governmental functions are carried on by human beings. Human beings do not operate in a vacuum; their actions are determined by the influence of social relationships, a fusion of environmental and hereditary forces both of a pro- and of anti-social character. Since democracy in the American view is synonymous with the public weal, the struggle for a democratic control of the social environment finds its expression in efforts directed at thwarting and repressing the action of antisocial forces and antidemocratic influences.

The influence of these forces on the life of the social organism is given due consideration in the utopian schemes of the past through the recognition of the necessity of the control of antisocial tendencies or of their complete eradication. In particular, antisocial tendencies arising from the abuse of the power of property were looked upon with apprehension by most, if not all, of the proponents of idealistic schemes of social organization. The views of the utopians of how to contend with the problem of neutralizing these tendencies run all the way from suggestions that the property instinct be controlled to outright communization of all property, or as in the case of Marxism—to the socialization of the means of production and distribution.

The significance of the influence exerted by the power of property on social relationships was forcefully recognized by two such totally dissimilar mentalities as those of Plato and of Karl Marx holding widely divergent social views and separated in history.

To the problem presented by the disparity between the American anti-monopoly tradition and the actual development of the monopolistic power in our economic life we find an approach of great significance in the ideas of Plato concerning the relation between the people of the state and its administration. Marx, on the other hand, was not preoccupied with the problem of administration since the logical extension of his thoughts led to a classless society and the elimination of the institution of government as we conceive it. Plato considered the administrative problem as of crucial importance in an ideally ordered state and the qualities of administrator as of determining significance to the fulfillment of its social philosophy.

Although Plato belonged to the slave owning aristocracy and his Republic was founded on a rigid delineation of social classes, he was much concerned with the factor of objective reasoning and logic in administration within the framework of the social structure of his utopian republic. The Kings-Philosophers who were to rule his ideal state were set apart from society from early childhood and were trained in such a way as to acquire the habit of following solely the dictates of reason, free from environmental influences. Their segregation from society was to render them immune from bias, from preconceived opinions and from prejudiced judgments, the unavoidable accompaniments of life in an environment hewn out of human relationships.

The powerful role of the property instinct in the formation of preconceived ideas was recognized by Plato in that the rulers of his Republic, the Kings-Philosophers, were to possess no personal property. Most of Plato's successors among the utopians, particularly the utopian socialists, were concerned about the adverse influence of the property instinct on human actions, while Marx considered it as a determining factor in the life of society. Those whose thoughts were directed towards furthering human happiness through a rearrangement of social relationships, recognized the fact that under one form or another, disturbing influences arising either out of the nature of man or out of the peculiarities of the social structure act as a deterrent to the realization of an ideally balanced order.

In enacting the Sherman Antitrust Act and other similar legislation, American democracy has recognized the role which property in its antisocial aspects plays in hindering the fulfillment of altruistic social aims and aspirations. The guiding thought of anti-monopoly legislation is to foster the development of the pro-social phases of the institution of property as they manifest themselves in a free economy.

However, the growth of concentrated private economic power in this country shows that the democratic legislative safeguards aimed at checking the antisocial tendencies of the ownership of property have not always worked successfully in connection with the laws which were enacted to ensure a free economic order in the nation. Two possibilities present themselves — in addition to the fact that these laws may be deficient in some particulars — either the governmental functions are not carried out efficiently in the field of anti-monopoly activities or these activities are subject to influences of an antisocial character. Since the latter possibility is of a deep significance, it is upon the problem of objectivity in the execution of legislative, administrative and judicial functions that the study of the strange phenomenon of the development of monopoly in a nation of a stalwart anti-monopoly tradition must be centered.

As in everything that concerns social phenomena the question of objective reasoning and logic with reference to antitrust activities must be considered from a teleological point of view, from the angle of what the aims and objectives of a social conglomerate are, viewed in the light of its ideals. Plato's Kings-Philosophers were trained to be objective but only within the framework of his rigidly delineated class structure. In present day America, objectivity by the governing bodies is to be exercised within the limits delineated by the concept of capitalist democracy. Which side will win — free will as expressive of the chosen American goal of competitive capitalism, or fatalism as expressive of the anti-American forces aligned with monopoly capitalism—is largely a question of the initiation and enforcement of laws through reason and logic, and of their administration and interpretation. The struggle between fatalism and free will as it is taking place in American economics reduces itself to the question of whose influence is preponderant on the organs of government — that of the pro-social forces represented by the original American concept of capitalist democracy, or the antisocial forces represented by monopoly capitalism.

The source of the struggle between fatalism as represented by monopoly and the national free will as represented by capitalistic democracy lies in the conflict of opposing interests. Unless the problem of monopoly is considered from this angle, its role in history cannot be properly evaluated. It resolves itself into the question of deciding not only what action should be taken on the basis of scientific data but of examining the relative power of conflicting interests as this power bears on the application of these data to the solution of the problem of monopoly. The factor of power plays a considerable part in upsetting the analyses and conclusions concerned with the identification of causal sequences as an essential prerequisite of social action. The problem of monopoly becomes to a large extent a problem of contending powers. The power of a democratic people aspiring to establish a competitive access to economic resources is pitted against the power of monopoly to hold — and to expand — its domination of these resources.

In the utopian schemes and in Marxism the question of power bears directly upon property. In the American ideology, however, power does not bear upon property itself but upon use of property. It is concerned with the antisocial use of property, which stems from the misuse of the profit motive originating in the power of concentrated business. This power shows itself in various forms, either as direct coercion or, more frequently, in subtle and indirect methods of eliminating competition. But it finds a fertile field for action in the areas in which the crucial battle against monopoly is waged, namely, in the Congress of the United States, in which it acts through group pressures. It also utilizes to its advantage the inadequacy of the existing court procedure to deal with the intricate phases of modern business organization.

Two thousand five hundred years ago the Greek philosopher Plato proclaimed the need for reason and logic in the administration of state affairs; over one hundred and seventy years ago the founders of this republic sought to give the American people wide opportunities to control their social environment through reason and logic. Yet, after all these years we find that in the central sphere of our government, that of legislation and law enforcement, a situation obtains in which reason and logic are all too frequently sacrificed to the pressure of special business interests at variance with our social and economic ideals. The pressure groups representing these interests are in a superior strategic position inasmuch as business, or rather that sector of it which is commonly known as "big business" and which occupies a dominant position in our economy presents, as a rule, a unified front with respect to legislation and law enforcement. On the other hand, the government in a democratic representative state is, by its very nature, not in a position to follow a consistent and united course of action in controversial matters affecting diverse interests.

According to Blaisdell, several factors are responsible for the lack of unity in government. First, there is the geographical representation in the legislative bodies. This representation is based on the "assumption that people living in a certain area share in a general way the interests of their neighbors." [1]

This widely accepted assumption "is unjustified, if not actually false," [2] particularly if the change from local manufacture to the present day industry of national proportions and interdependence is considered. Among other factors contributing to the lack of consistency and unity in government are: the political representation which "is secured through the party system which involves compromise at the very start"; the relatively short terms of Congressmen and administrative officials and the lack of a unified philosophy with regard to social and economic problems. "Most important of all the factors in favor of business, however, are its resources — not so much because of their size, important as that is, as because of the circumstances surrounding their use. The extraordinary concentration of ownership in the 250 largest corporations, and the even greater concentration of control, enormously increase their mobility and effectiveness." [3]

It is this superior position of great corporations that presents the most serious problem in attempts to deal with the concentration of economic power.

---

[1] Donald C. Blaisdell, *Economic Power and Political Pressures*, TNEC Monograph No. 26, pp. 1-2.
[2] *Ibid.*, p. 2.   [3] *Ibid.*, p. 19.

CHAPTER XII

Power Legislation and Monopoly

The violation of the principle of a rational consideration of legislative bills stands out strikingly in the enactment of laws which provide for the exemption of particular industries and economic functions from the operation of anti-monopoly laws. A comparatively recent example of such legislative action is presented by the enactment by the 80th Congress of the Reed-Bulwinkle Bill. This action reveals an instance of a successful legislative effort to undermine the capitalism of free enterprise against every consideration of reason and logic as conditioned by the American concept of free enterprise. This law concerns the railroads — an enterprise which is of paramount importance to a highly interdependent economy such as ours. The Reed-Bullwinkle law strikes at the heart of free competition by depriving the federal courts of their jurisdiction over transportation rates.

Transportation rates, in a nation-wide, interdependent economy like ours, are the life-blood of the economic life. As President Truman told Congress, "Transportation rates affect the cost of goods as they move through each phase of production — from raw materials, through finished products, to the consumers. Power to control transportation rates is the power to influence the competitive success or failure of other business."[1]

The control of transportation rates has always been sought by those who control the railroads—namely, the investment bankers. Through the Association of American Railroads, the railroad corporations succeeded some years ago in having placed in a committee of directors the final authority for filing western rates with the Interstate Commerce Commission.

The legality of this procedure was challenged in two suits filed in federal courts charging the Association of American Railroads with violating the Sherman Antitrust Act. The State of Georgia charged the Association with freight discrimination against the South. The Department of Justice accused J. P. Morgan and Company, Kuhn Loeb and Company, and the Association of a monopolistic conspiracy to determine freight rates and to prevent the devolopment of states west of the Mississippi.

The Supreme Court gave support to these prosecutions by ruling that rate-fixing destroyed the "freedom of action"[1] envisaged by the

Interstate Commerce Commission Act. The Association of American Railroads then prepared, and Congress passed, the Reed-Bulwinkle Bill, designed to eliminate the jurisdiction of the federal courts over transportation rates. The President vetoed the bill but Congress enacted it over his veto. The law, as it stands now, legalizes the elimination of competition from the vital transportation industry and gives the railroad corporations the power to set prices and to control the introduction of new equipment.

Legislative approval of the violations of the principles of free competition is embodied in other federal laws, notably in the Tydings-Miller Amendment to the Sherman Antitrust Act, and in the Webb-Pomerene Act. The Tydings-Miller Amendment exempts wholesalers and retailers in interstate commerce from the operation of the provisions of the Sherman Act with respect to price-fixing. It legalizes resale-price maintenance laws on commodities sold in interstate commerce. It legalizes, at wholesale and retail levels, price-fixing practices which cost consumers millions of dollars each year in food and drug costs. The repeal of this law is urged by the Department of Justice and by the Federal Trade Commission. The interesting fact in connection with this law is that it was passed (in 1927) through the devious means of a rider to the District of Columbia appropriations bill.

Legalized monopoly was also given strong encouragement in the Webb-Pomerene Act, the repeal of which is urged by both the Senate Small Business Committee and the Department of Justice. This act was intended to permit small concerns to join together for export trade operations in order to match the power of European cartels. In practice, the Senate Small Business Committee found that it has encouraged world-wide cartelization, the growth of monopoly controls and the elimination of small concerns.

The most conspicuous instance of the power of special interests overriding reason and logic in the matter of antitrust legislation, is presented by the passage of Section 7 to the Clayton Act and the long futile efforts to eliminate it when its nefarious effects became self-evident. It was not until 1950 that this section was amended to make the act effective in forestalling mergers.

This section was adopted by Congress in 1914, avowedly to strengthen the Sherman Antitrust Act in preventing monopolistic combinations. It prohibits a corporation from acquiring the capital stock of another if such action leads to monopoly or elimination of competition. But the act did not prohibit the purchase of assets or the merger of properties. Possibly it was thought that it would have an automatic influence on preventing the acquisition of assets. This may be the most charitable interpretation of the motives behind the enactment of this section of the Clayton Act. It is difficult to fathom the reason the acquisition of assets was not prohibited as well as that of the capital stock.

Events proved the fallacy of the line of reasoning, whatever this may have been, which the framers of the section followed in enacting it. The fallacy was brought to light by corporation lawyers who "contrived ways to do legally what the laws forbid them to do." [2] They found sympathy in a court which "looked to the letter, not the intent of the law — considered the form, not the effect of the lawyers' stratagems. Ways were found to circumvent section 7, and as a result of a favorable court decision this portion of the Clayton Act was emasculated." [2]

The methods by which this was done were described in detail by the Temporary National Economic Committee. The corporation could either acquire control of a competitor through the purchase of its voting stock and thereby use the stock to obtain the physical assets, or it might purchase the factory equipment or good-will of the competitor. As David Lynch points out, these methods "use the illegal purchase of stocks in order to achieve the legally permissible acquisition of assets." [3]

These methods were given legal sanction through decisions in court cases which were brought before the Supreme Court. They involved Swift and Company, the Thatcher Manufacturing Company, and the Arrow-Hart-Hegeman Electric Company. In all these cases the company illegally purchased the stock of a competitor and then proceeded to acquire control of the property. "In each case the Federal Trade Commission ordered the respondent to divest itself of both the assets and the stock, since an order merely to divest itself of the stock would be an empty gesture and a mockery." [4]

The lower court sustained the order of the Commission, but despite the clear-cut reasoning on which the order of the Commission was based, the Supreme Court, upon appeal, reversed the decision of the lower court. The courts held that although the Clayton Act had been violated by the acquisition of stock ownership and, although through this method the respondent had acquired control of assets of its competitor, the Federal Trade Commission was powerless to do anything about it. Inasmuch as the companies had "legally" gained control of the assets prior to action by the Federal Trade Commission, the latter had acted beyond its authority to require the company to divest itself of control. The Court was divided in each case, four justices, including the Chief Justice, dissenting.

Badly as this decision violates the laws of reason and logic, the most amazing thing in connection with this section of the Clayton Act is that Congress has consistently for years refused to amend the act so as to remedy a situation which cried to heaven for lack of reason, logic, justice and simple common sense — especially when there is considered the availability of comprehensive data gathered on this subject by various agencies, notably by a subcommittee of the Committee of the Judiciary of the House of Representatives of the Seventy-Ninth Congress. In 1941, the Temporary National Economic Committee, after exhaustive hearings and investigations, recommended that "Section 7 of the Clayton Act be amended so as to include within its prohibition the acquisition of assets of competitors under conditions applicable to stock under existing law." [5]

A more recent example of legislative proposals which operate against the letter and the spirit of free enterprise is concerned with the introduction of several so-called "fair trade" bills in the 1952 Congressional session.

Fair trade laws enacted in 45 states contained a so-called "non-signer" clause permitting a manufacturer to bind all retailers to the prices set in an agreement with anyone of them. The United States Supreme Court outlawed this power in May 1951 on the ground that Congress had never intended to let Fair Traders have it. A new bill was introduced at the 1952 session of Congress which would allow manufacturers to force all retailers to observe their minimum prices. Although both the Department of Justice Anti-trust division and the Fair Trade Commission were vigorously opposed to it, a judiciary subcommittee which held hearings on a similar bill, decided tentatively to recommend the bill which also contained the non-signer clause. However, the chairman of this subcommittee, Congressman Emanuel Celler, issued a statement in connection with a bill which he introduced to prohibit loss leader selling. In this statement Congressman Celler criticized "fair trade" laws pointing out that they "artificially impose on our competitive system a scale of prices which do not reflect healthy retail competition". In Mr. Celler's view "the fair trade bills are nothing more than price fixing bills which are designed to enrich certain retailers by fixing prices upward and not downward. The result is — the public takes a rooking". [6]

The enactment, under the pressure of special interests, of laws exempting certain areas of our economic activities from anti-monopoly legislation constitutes in the last analysis a legalization of the misuse of the profit motive. Such exemptions deprive important economic sectors of the application of the American concept of an unobstructed working of the profit motive as conditioning a just and efficient functioning of our economy from a physical as well as a social point of view. By enacting laws such as the Reed-Bulwinkle Act, the Tydings-Miller Amendment, and the Webb-Pomerene Act, and by emasculating the thought underlying the passage of the Clayton Act, the various Congressional sessions which were responsible acted as unconscious agents of those antisocial forces which, originating in the misuse of the profit motive, are undermining the capitalism of free enterprise. Through these enactments we acknowledge that, in stead of controlling social forces in the direction of a free competitive society, we are allowing these forces to dominate us.

The pressure of special interests on antitrust legislation indicates that the quintessence of the struggle between monopoly and economic freedom is power versus reason understood as a true perception of the causal interplay of social phenomena as it either furthers or hinders the fulfillment of our economic ideal. Antitrust laws are basically the manifestations of the American concept of the control of the social environment through reason. The theory which is implicit in the provisions of such legislation is interwoven with the meaning of democracy as implying conscious mass action to give substance to the democratic ideal of economic freedom. The actual contest in this field is between government and those private interests which are intent upon wielding economic power, and, where necessary, political control to achieve their purpose.

Of a concern equal to that of pressure on legislation is the pressure on administrative agencies charged with the enforcement of laws. There is no branch of government activities that escapes the attention of pressure groups. A subject of prime interest to organized groups are the appropriation bills. "These provide a constantly recurring battleground for the forces opposing and favoring the various departments and agencies. One way of emasculating an agency whose operations are distasteful or inimical to certain groups is to cut its appropriation to a point where it cannot carry on its program. Certain departments or divisions of an agency may be cut out, or a whole agency may be starved out by drastic slashes. The repeated attempts to cut the appropriations for relief work, as well as for the National Youth Administration, the Securities and Exchange Commission, the National Labor Relations Board, the Justice Department's Antitrust Division and so forth, are examples of this policymaking in appropriations."[7]

Examples of group pressures abound in the modern literature on the subject and it would be superfluous to discuss them over again. Let us cite, however, one interesting case of such pressure which, although it goes back a number of years, "is according to Blaisdell curiously contemporary in its approach."⁸ This case concerns an attempt by Congress to uncover monopolistic practices in the meat packing industry. "A House investigation of the Institute of Meat Packers which was under fire in 1916 was sidetracked by the efforts of the Institute. Three years later, by having a resolution introduced in the Senate to investigate the so-called socialist members of the Federal Trade Commission, the Institute diverted attention from a Commission report showing monopolistic practices among the big meat packers."⁹

The pressure of special interests upon the government to force it to adopt a line of action in contradiction to the idea of free competition would bear out Marx's theory that government in a capitalist country plays the role of a Board of Directors of the ruling economic groups, particularly if account is taken of the several instances of anti-competitive measures enacted into law. However, there are trends developing in this country which point to a nascent awakening on the part of the public to the consequences of the encroachments of monopoly on our economic freedom. These trends, which will be discussed in the final chapter of this book, are manifested in the greater opportunities afforded the Antitrust Division of the U.S. Department of Justice and the Federal Trade Commission in the enforcement of anti-monopoly legislation; in the increasing number of court decisions upholding the government in antitrust actions; in the comprehensive investigation of the concentration of economic power conducted by Congressional committees and, particularly, in the refusal by the 81st Congress to enact a law legalizing the principal features of the basing-point system despite tremendous pressure which was brought to bear upon Congressmen by the interests which were affected by the decision of the court which upheld the Federal Trade Commission in its action against this monopolistic practice. These tendencies, despite occasional setbacks, coupled with the growth of social consciousness in the nation as it is manifested in other fields of our national life, reveal the hidden democratic strength of our national psychology and presage the strong probability that the Marxian concept of the peculiar role of government under capitalism may prove as erroneous as the Marxian forecast of the development of a revolutionary workers' psychology as an inevitable consequence of industrial concentration.

Labor and Agriculture

The growth of concentrated economic power and the development of subtle practices of monopoly implementation have generated in the society at large an antisocial spirit which is often diverting into antisocial channels organized efforts to improve the condition of labor. Under the pressure of conditions generated by industrial monopolies, certain trade-unions, notably the building trades, are resorting to tactics designed to restrict production in their spheres of activity. These practices are prompted by the fear of losing jobs; by the feeling of insecurity resulting from the monopolistic policy of scarcity planning. In this connection it should be considered that the business and industrial monopolies developed on an extensive scale long before certain sections of labor embarked upon a policy of anti-competitive practices.

This, however, does not justify the reprehensible practices of some unions, such as that known as "feather-bedding" and many other antisocial practices which constitute deliberate attempts to create unnecessary jobs and, in general, to take unfair advantage of employers and consumers. Such practices are contrary to the basic philosophy of trade-unionism.

That such practices are not representative of the labor movement as a whole is evidenced by the social philosophy of the Congress of Industrial Organizations (the C.I.O.) as given expression in the July, 1949, issue of its official organ, *The Economic Outlook*. In an article entitled "Action on Unemployment" the organization advocates, among other socially inspired measures, vigorous action against monopoly to "promote high production at reasonable price and profit levels." It also went on record as demanding "grant loans to new and small business, and for necessary expansion of productive capacity in basic industries in line with future needs of full employment economy." That these are not mere words is shown by the struggle which Walter Reuther, President of the United Automobile Workers, waged against the plans of the steel interests to reduce steel production so as not to risk their profits.

What is true of labor is equally true of farmers so far as an artificial support of farm prices and other methods of direct assistance to farmers are concerned, even if they are at variance with sound economics. It is the same story of a monopoly dominated environment reinforced by the concentration of economic power in the distribution of farm products.

This was vividly brought out by the Secretary of Agriculture Charles F. Brannan in his testimony before the Celler committee on the study of monopoly power:

"The farmer has long been pitted against economic giants and has had to fight constantly for his freedom. It is a never-ending struggle.

"It is still true to a considerable degree that the farmer has to accept what is offered when he sells his products and that he has to pay what is asked when he buys.

"This is another way of saying that whether the farmer is buying or selling he is confronted with concentrated economic power greater than his own . . .

"A basic reason for price-support programs is to give the farmer greater independence in choosing the time and the price at which he is willing to sell. The Congress probably would never have legislated price-support programs were it not for the fact that industry has cut production to maintain price while the farmer traditionally has gone on producing while his prices went farther and farther down out of line with industrial prices.

"A basic reason for programs assuring agricultural credit has been the power of financial concerns to deny the farmer access to the reasonable credit terms he had to have for his very existence.

"A basic reason for the rural electrification program is to circumvent the concentrated economic power which was used for so long to deny farmers the modern benefits of electric power."[10]

It should be pointed out in this connection that the present day large scale farmers' marketing organizations are handicapped in that market outlets for most farm products are controlled by a relatively few large corporations.

While hoping that in the normal course of our social evolution the forces of democracy will make a substantial progress towards the development of a normally functioning economy, the present situation calls for government assistance to provide the farmers and workers with an opportunity to make an effective demand for each other's products — an opportunity of which they are deprived by the impediments to the efficient operation of our economic mechanism. It is this consideration that explains the activities of the labor and *bona fide* farm organizations which work through their own pressure groups to further favorable labor and farm legislation as an offsetting force to the Big Business pressure groups.

[1] *New Republic*, January 10, 1949.
[2] David Lynch, *The Concentration of Economic Power*, p. 280.
[3] *Ibid.*, p. 280.   [4] *Ibid.*, p. 281.
[5] *Final Report and Recommendations of the Temporary National Economic Committee*, pp. 38-39.
[6] Statement by Congressman Emanuel Celler, press release March 11, 1952.
[7] Donald C. Blaisdell, *Economic Power and Political Pressures*, TNEC Monograph No. 21, p. 59.
[8] *Ibid.*, p. 58.   [9] *Ibid.*, p. 59.
[10] *Study of Monopoly Power*, Hearings before the Subcommittee on Study of Monopoly Power of the Committee on the Judiciary, House of Representatives, Eighty-first Congress; Serial No. 14, Part 1, pp. 163-164.

CHAPTER XIII

Power Litigation and Monopoly

Under our system of government the ultimate contest between the pro-social and the antisocial forces as this contest revolves around antitrust legislation takes place in the courts. This contest follows the rules of the established court procedure. Upon the objectivity of these rules depends to a large extent a proper correlation between these antagonistic forces.

The peculiar feature of our process of law in its relation to antitrust court suits is that it makes it possible for the defendants of superior financial power to take advantage of antiquated rules of procedure and thus hinder a smooth and speedy court action to the detriment of the government's antitrust cases.

In its essence, our legal procedure is based on a rule of English common law, that of restraint, which was established in the days when economic relations revolved largely around local trading. The distinctive characteristic of that economy was a definiteness in industrial and commercial relations. In the days of self-sufficing farming, for instance, when trade was confined to transactions within a locality, the seller and the buyer were in close contact with each other. Moreover, the numbers of both buyers and sellers within a locality was limited. Any attempt at what the law calls "restraints" was quickly noticed. Such an attempt showed itself in a definite form. Consequently, restraints were few in numbers, and when they were uncovered, the simple form in which they were revealed made the task of applying the law rather easy. This was true not only in agriculture but in cities as well. The domestic type of industry was marked by simplicity in the relations between buyers and sellers. The law of restraints dealt with concrete, easily recognizable relations.

As the economic life of the nation evolved, as large scale production of national proportions, with its intricate network of distribution spread over the land and replaced local industry and trading, the law of restraint was confronted with a complicated situation. Conditions appeared which were basically different from those under which the common law had developed. In the old days the prevalent market was the open spot market. Goods were generally bought and sold with reference to supplies actually or nearly so at hand within a given period of time. With the growth of economic concentration the open market gave way to a situation which was not fathomed in the days of domestic industry and self-sufficient agriculture. As Walton Hamilton points out, "Questions once left to the free play of buying and selling came to invite personal or corporate discretion and it was inevitable that, as the governor of industrial activity, the open market should be supplemented, compromised and superseded. The corporation often forsook the spot-market for long term contracts or integration. An automobile concern, by a series of covenants which run for years ahead, takes conscious steps to assure itself of adequate supplies of all needful parts and materials. An oil company, whose domain stretches from well to filling station, establishes a single discretion over an entire productive process."[1] These changes in the direction of interdependence and intricacy of marketing functions developed in one way or another various practices: "a discount structure, a classification of customers, a basing-point system, bureaus of estimate, market information surveys and so on."[2] These and various other practices came to replace the simple selling and buying transactions of old. Their characteristic feature is that "they all tend to deflect the unbridled forces of competition."[3] The open market now "performs its office within an impinging network of institutions."[4]

With the development of antitrust legislation the men at the head of the great corporations came to be confronted with a grave problem. The success of the Antitrust Act would have meant the breaking up of their industrial empires. The unhampered working of the principle of free competition would have curtailed their profit figures. They were in a quandary. "As good citizens they were concerned to be law-abiding; as able business men they were loath to refrain from activities which were to their advantage. Where values clash a formula must be found — one which will reconcile the pursuit of gain with the prohibition against monopoly."[5] The real aim sought was to preserve opportunities for the misuse of the profit motive while observing the proprieties of competitive practices.

As a result of the struggle between profit and conscience, "old ends came to be served with modulated means; coercion was dissipated into a discipline of gentle reminders; crude restraint was subdued into a fine art."[6] The old crude methods of piracy were replaced, as was noted earlier, by subtle and sophisticated methods of the new type of monopoly implementation. The result showed itself in a variety of practices such as price leadership, the basing point system, trade associations, the development of "cost formulas" for the price of various goods, etc. Invisible collusion "under the guise of the meeting of congenial minds" replaced conspiracy.

Considering the requirement to prove restraint, as it is developed in the common law, the government, in the prosecution of antitrust cases, is confronted basically with the problem of translating the invisible into the visible; or, as Walton Hamilton says, "the impersonal into the personal." The court demands the proofs of an "overt" act. Every item must live up to "the rules of evidence." But it should be borne in mind that the code of evidence as we have it now "grew out of concern with ordinary cases in tort, contract and crime. Its exactions pivoted upon a simple, easily identified act, clean cut in intent and effect, the deed of an individual or a small group of individuals."[7] A discussion of market conditions at a friendly meeting which leads to one conclusion as to price is not sufficient proof of conspiracy. Actual collusion must be shown either directly or by circumstantial evidence. The more intricate are the pricemaking forces in an industry, the more difficult it is to prove direct collusion or adduce circumstantial evidence.

As industry grew and developed to its present proportions, the task of a simple, easy identification of an act, clean cut in intent and effect, became very elusive.

"The paper industry carries on through a durable agreement among gentlemen. Since no others are admitted to the closed club, a ceremonial meeting of minds would serve little purpose. Stability is maintained through ways of action taken for granted. In lead pencils and fertilizers 'quality standards' have been used to do the pioneer work. A multitude of brands has been reduced to a few grades, plainly marked, easily identified. The resulting simplicity invites a uniform price structure, makes departure easy to detect, enables 'persuasion' to be brought to bear upon erring members."[8] This presents law enforcement officials with an arduous task. A governmental prosecuting agency must dig out evidence to prove that certain phenomena constitute collusion. And even when evidence is forthcoming there follows a battle over it as to admissability, relevancy, competence and exclusion. In their efforts to win an antitrust case the attorneys for the defense often carry the idea of the protection of the rights of the individual to extremes. This is made possible by the fact that the court procedure which is used in antitrust cases was shaped to deal with such elementary wrongs as slander, fraud, assault, theft, arson, seduction, manslaughter. "It seeks to protect the accused against gossip, rumor, surmise, inference" and the court limits testimony to "direct, straightforward, authenticated statement . . . . its norms of admission, relevancy, competence, exclusion lie far from the area in which legal combats over the patterns of industry are staged." [9]

Considering the intricacy of modern courtroom procedure as well as of modern business phenomena, the facts relating to the question of evidence condition the character of a lawsuit as a duel, as a legal combat. The question becomes not so much one of unraveling facts as of presenting data in such a way as to impress the judge and the jury, irrespective of the actual value of these data. The trial becomes not a process to discover the truth but a battle where anything is considered fair if it helps win the case. The question becomes one not of convincing the judge and the jury on the basis of actual facts in the light of rational interpretation but to interpret the facts so as to make the jury believe what the attorneys want them to believe. Considering the intricacies of present day large scale business trans-- actions with their numerous ramifications and the intangible factors which determine these transactions, the question of interpretation of facts is conditioned more by dialectical ability than by actual merits.

Then there are the long, sometimes interminable tactics of chal- lenging the evidence, demanding that it be not admitted and explain- ing the reasons for this demand; leaving it to the judge whether the demand should be sustained or overruled.

As a matter of fact "the rules of evidence are vague enough to allow considerable latitude" [10] on the part of the judges.

But then another problem arises — that of the personality and temperament of the judge. One judge may exclude evidence because it does not conform to the strict rules meant for much simpler cases of litigation. Another judge, of more broadminded tendencies, will be less strict in admitting evidence. He will tend to favor what is offered, and exclude only when he clearly must. The antitrust cases are thus left to chance. This makes of antitrust enforcement a hap- hazard venture into the unknown instead of a conscious and reasoned program of action aimed at neutralizing the forces which militate against the realization of the basic tenets of our economic philosophy.

The spirit of the democratic way of life is to solve social problems in an evolutionary manner through reasoning based on facts. In disputes between capital and labor, a revolutionary solution is being more and more frequently averted by means of an unrestricted presentation of the full facts by the contending parties to impartial arbitrators. In such cases the conflict between capital and labor is settled through reasoning based on facts — on evidence presented at will without any restrictions or long drawn out battles as to the propriety of their admission.

But the contradictory situations resulting from the contrast between the rules which govern court procedure and the problems which are involved in antitrust cases, are pregnant with opportunities for the exercise of power instead of reasoning. Objective consideration of the pros and cons gives way to a battle of wits, to "trial by combat" in the words of Walton Hamilton. And in this combat the advantage is on the side of those contestants who possess the superior sinews of war, i.e., the resources which make delay possible — irrespective of the personal ability and talents of the counsel on either side.

The nature of these sinews of war is shown, notably, in the need of securing data from the files of the defendants. "The crux of the matter [in antitrust cases]," according to Walton Hamilton, "is access to files."[11] The circumstances surrounding access to files make the efforts at obtaining documentary evidence a question of controversy from the start. It is a foretaste of the combative nature of the court action which is to follow. "Like the action at law which it heralds, it [the securing of data] is freighted with circumstances, request and answer, limitation and definition of the issue, and delay."[12] The delivery of the material contained in the files is delayed for as long as possible under various pretexts.

"Always some time elapses between the first appearance of antitrust investigators and the granting or withholding of material. The initial call is an event which officials may turn to the advantage of their corporation. It is, in effect, an announcement of an impending antitrust suit and a warning to the company to regiment its activities for defense . . . . Difficulties are discovered which must be resolved; simple requests are made complex and require clarification; an attempt is made to wear the question out before it ever comes to a decision. A series of ingeniously timed delays may protract the issue for months or even years."[13]

Delay is a favorite weapon of the defense and the greater the resources it possesses, the more delays it contrives to engineer. When asked for documentary material a small concern usually yields easily, the more so as it may be ignorant of the extent of the power possessed by the investigators. But a large concern engages in a complicated fight. It has an informed legal staff. "The usual technique is to play along and to defer hostile engagement. The initial call at the offices of the corporation frequently defers decision; a discreet interval must be given for a consideration of the request. The company's attorney is occupied with court work, is out of town on business, has just departed for the first vacation in years. In a matter that may have legal consequences, the officials do not feel free to act without consulting him."[14]

When the case reaches the courtroom it assumes the aspect of a major engagement. This is brilliantly brought out in the following description:

"The ancient spirit of trial by combat broods over the whole affair. It is manifest in a series of skirmishes which precede the general engagement. An indictment in a criminal case is invariably met with demurrer and motion to quash. If the judge resolutely denies, request is put in for a bill of particulars. If the demurrer is sustained, appeal will be taken, usually all the way up to the United States Supreme Court; and only after an ultimate victory on points at law can the case come to trial. A plea in equity is regularly met by a long answer, categorical denial, and a prayer to dismiss the complaint. Along the whole course interlocutory motions — some of them subject to appeal — will be made, contested, amended, reargued, decided while the real issue abides its time in the offing. If one side shifts to the procedural front, the other must meet it there; ;and the techniques possessed by the defense are adequate to a real game of obstruction. In an antitrust suit, where large sums may be available to beat off an attack, the older devices of the law are mere primitive elements out of which 'the higher procrastination' has been refined. No attorney of skill would be content to create two issues where one had been before; at least half a dozen would be essential to satisfy his professional pride. Procedure becomes a buttress against substantive attack; behind its fortifications the defense digs in for a long siege." [15]

In this court battle the advantage is definitely with the side that possesses the necessary resources enabling it to live through delays, procrastinations, interminable juggling of the rules with respect to evidence, and so on. The resources for defense even in a petty industry vastly exceed those of the prosecution. In a speech before the antitrust section of the New York State Bar Association, U.S. Supreme Court Justice Tom C. Clark, the then Attorney General of the United States, called attention to the high cost involved in the average anti-trust case for the government. Considering this cost, the appropriations allotted by Congress to the enforcement of antitrust legislation are pitifully inadequate. "Not until its fiftieth year was as much as $1,000,000 appropriated to the purposes of the Sherman Act. For more than a decade no separate staff was charged with its enforcement; and when, in 1903, antitrust became a division in the Department of Justice, it was given only half a million dollars, to be expended at the rate of $100,000 a year over a period of 5 years. Between 1908 and 1935 the appropriation varied between $100,000 and $300,000. In 1936, the figure was increased to $435,000; in 1939, to about $800,000, and for the fiscal years of 1940 and 1941 to $1,300,000 and $1,325,000."[16] In 1949 it was $3,571,700 and in 1950 $3,864,938. In 1951 it dropped to $3,750,000.

These figures present a pitiful picture when considered in relation to the duties imposed upon the Antitrust division. This agency "must enforce the law by apprehending violations, presenting lawbreakers to the courts, carrying cases through the mazes of protracted litigation. Then, when the last court has spoken, it must follow up judgments and make sure judicial decrees become everyday realities . . . The contrast between the miniature staff on duty and the enormity of the job to be done speaks for itself,"[17] the more so when we consider the intricacies and wide ramifications of the present day industrial structure which presuppose expert economic analysis of a wide range in preparation for an antitrust suit.

The pecuniary resources of the defendant, as contrasted with those of the antitrust division, are reinforced by their strategic position in the industry. This comes out with particular clarity in the case of witnesses called by the government. An important factor in the willingness of the witness to testify is fear of reprisals on the part of the industry, which may assume varied and effective forms. "The friendly witness would, if he could, tell his story simply, directly, with corroborative detail. He is constrained by personal interest to tell no more than that which against every doubt stands out as the truth."[18]

The contradiction between the rules which govern a suit in court in antitrust cases on the one hand, and the intricate economic problems which are involved in such cases lead, in the words of Walton Hamilton, to "a neat situation in which logic and reason are beyond the reach of the law."[19] A court suit reflects the situation as it obtains in the nation at large. Antitrust legislation embodies the thought of a logical and reasoning effort to prevent monopoly from dominating our economic structure. The fact that monopoly has attained the proportions of major significance in our economy means that, as in the court room so in our economic life, logic and reason tend to be beyond the reach of social action.

Considering the authoritative position of the courts in our scheme of government, court action not only reflects this tendency but intensifies it. A court case decided on any other basis than logic and reason gives that much encouragement to antisocial forces. Court cases and decisions may either weaken or strengthen these forces. In court, logic and reason are often thwarted by forces which have no relation to the merits of a case. In life, they are thwarted by forces inimical to the American concept of private enterprise operating under competitive conditions.

When reason and logic recede, blind forces override efforts at a pragmatic solution of the problem of control of the social environment. From this point of view, the courts, in virtue of their role as arbiters of controversies in monopoly cases, occupy a strategic position in the question of whether our history will develop along revolutionary or evolutionary lines. Fortunately, there is evidence of a present tendency on the part of the courts towards the consideration of monopoly cases in the light of broad social philosophy, and for this development the stubborn and social-minded efforts of the Antitrust Division of the United States Department of Justice can claim a fair share of the credit.

Speaking of the Antitrust Division and also of the Federal Trade Commission, it is cause for wonderment that these agencies have accomplished as much as they have, in view of the circumstances surrounding court litigation with their palpably insufficient resources as compared with the resources that concentrated economic power can bring into court cases. This shows that, despite appearances, the pro-social forces have developed considerable vitality. In this lies largely our hope for the future of economic freedom in this country.

[1] Walton Hamilton, *Antitrust in Action,* Temporary National Economic Committee, Monograph No. 16, pp. 12-13.

[2] *Ibid.,* p. 13.
[3] *Ibid.,* p. 13.
[4] *Ibid.,* p. 13.
[5] *Ibid.,* p. 13.
[6] *Ibid.,* p. 13.
[7] *Ibid.,* p. 61.
[8] *Ibid.,* p. 14.
[9] *Ibid.,* p. 61.
[10] *Ibid.,* p. 61.
[11] *Ibid.,* p. 50.
[12] *Ibid.,* p. 50.
[13] *Ibid.,* pp. 50-51.
[14] *Ibid.,* p. 49.
[15] *Ibid.,* p. 60.
[16] *Ibid.,* p. 23.
[17] *Ibid.,* p. 23.
[18] *Ibid.,* p. 48.
[19] *Ibid.,* p. 68.

CHAPTER XIV

Anti-Monopoly Legislation and a Congenial Social Atmosphere

Economic problems arise in consequence of the action of antisocial forces. The reality of the monopoly problem indicates that the antisocial forces as they manifest themselves in the growth of monopoly have been more potent than the pro-social forces as these are symbolized by the efforts to promote economic freedom. The possibility of the solution of the monopoly problem centers around the question of whether social trends are developing a congenial social atmosphere for the action of the pro-social forces. Specifically speaking, we are confronted with the task of neutralizing, through a strengthened antitrust legislation — the embodiment of the American tradition — the threat to the American democracy innate in monopoly capitalism.

The approach to the problem of what to do about the concentration of economic power must be guided by the thought that this power was brought to its present strength through the action of antisocial forces which found a free field of operation because of a comparative inactivity of counteracting pro-social forces. Consequently, any attempt at a solution of this problem must be considered in the light of the possibility of the pro-social forces gaining in strength at the expense of the antisocial forces. The prospects of a successful application to our economic life of the many valuable suggestions which are being made to meet the problem of monopoly are interwoven with the presence of a social climate congenial to the social concept legislation; a climate which would stimulate the pro-social forces of the capitalism of free enterprise in their struggle with the antisocial forces of monopoly capitalism. The essence of the struggle between these two sets of forces is that of power versus reason — not abstract reason but reason guided by the economic principles which form an integral part of the American social philosophy. Reason may indicate the right direction, but power through pressure on legislation and enforcement — the only means of social action in a democracy — prevents or impedes action.

Social Trends in American Society

In the struggle between the pro-social and the antisocial forces an important, if not crucial role is played by leadership. The burden of social progress is carried in the last analysis by leaders. But the struggle of even an ideal leadership is weakened by an indifferent or an inimical social atmosphere. Ever since the Sherman Antitrust Act was passed we had farsighted and courageous leadership in and out of legislative bodies which fought for the principles which form the foundation of this act. Its very passage shows that there was such a leadership at the time — over fifty years ago. And still the antitrust act was practically dormant* until the year 1936 when Thurman Arnold embarked upon its earnest enforcement which is continuing with an ever increasing forcefulness and greatly enlarged, although still woefully inadequate appropriations. The reason for the unprecedented progress of Arnold and his successors in the office of Chief of the Antitrust Division was, besides their personal qualities of leadership, the fact that they were working in the conditions of a more socially congenial atmosphere than that which prevailed before — an atmosphere in the absence of which the most powerful leadership is impotent.

Leadership does not operate in a vacuum. If the circumstances of time and place, as associated with lack of active and articulate public support, are unfavorable, the most ideal plans of action and the most competent leadership are of no avail. It is public support that creates a congenial social climate — a climate in which the pro-social forces operate with a degree of certainty of success against the antisocial forces. But when such a climate is present, leadership can go far in fortifying a congenial social atmosphere as is shown by the activities of the antitrust division of the United States Department of Justice and the Federal Trade Commission in stimulating greater interest and sympathy for legislative efforts to solve the problem of monopoly.

Legislation which operates in a congenial social atmosphere is that lever in social relationships analogous to the one which in the realm of physics enables a man to lift a stone beyond his strength. The conscious disciples of Karl Marx, such as the communists and the socialists contend that no legislation playing the part of that lever is of any value with respect to the problem of monopoly because of the power of the economic forces which drive us towards the destruction of capitalism. The unconscious adherents of this theory — the social defeatists in our midst — hold that neither legislation or anything else can break up economic concentration because there is no power that can stop the urge towards a mass economy. If this is the case then any consideration of the problem of reestablishing economic freedom is futile. Concentration and centralization of economic activities spell the death of our traditional concept of economic freedom.

The only alternatives to enforcing antitrust legislation are: either to let monopoly capitalism have full sway over us or to socialize the means of production and distribution which have come under its domination. In fact, the first alternative leads to the second. The almost complete cartelization of the economy of Great Britain led to the coming to power of the Labor Government with its attempted program of the socialization of the basic industries of the country. As to the other alternative — economic planning — which is heralded as a possible solution of our economic maladjustments, it rests largely upon the possibility of freeing our economy from monopolistic practices but it may lead to dictatorship.

The basic difference between the American tradition and socialism revolves around the question of individualism. In socialism the individual is subjugated to the collective, whereas the American social philosophy seeks to establish a proper balance between the interests of the individual and that of society.

Monopoly capitalism is also founded on the concept of individualism but of a variety known as rugged individualism which implies the rule of the strong and leads to the submergence of the individual in the collectivism of economic concentration. Rugged individualism played a decisive role in that period of American history when the momentous problem was the conquest of the frontier—the struggle with the inimical forces of nature. It is a beneficent force in the struggle with the physical environment. But when it was applied in the economic sphere it manifested itself in various anti-social ways, notably in the high-handed exploitation of workers and in the ruthless elimination of competitors in the early days of the formation of the great American trusts and also during the period between the two wars, the period of mergers and consolidations. In recent decades it has also assumed the more subtle form of monopolistic practices.

Opposed to this type of individualism is the concept of enlightened individualism which seeks to harmonize the interests of the individual with those of society. This concept is imbedded in the American tradition as it traces its origin to the social principles embodied in the Declaration of Independence and in the Constitution of the United States. It is expressed in the progress which social legislation has been making since the days of the depression of the thirties.

The concept of enlightened individualism flows logically from the association of the theory of individual freedom with the obligation which the preamble to the Declaration of Independence places on governments to secure the citizen the rights to "life, liberty and the pursuit of happiness." It is the expression of the social principle which was the keynote of the philosophy underlying the two great

liberating movements of the 18th century — the American Revolutionary War and the French Revolution of 1789 — the principle that
"the liberty of an individual ends where the liberty of another begins."
The realization of this principle is conditioned by the promotion of
"the general welfare" and the securing of "the blessings of liberty to
ourselves and our posterity" which the preamble to the Constitution
of the United States brings out as two of the several objects for the
attainment of which the Constitution was "ordained" and "established."
In the light of the principles proclaimed by the Declaration of Independence and the Constitution of the United States the individual is
considered in his relation to society; the fullest development of individual rights being interwoven with the consideration of public
welfare.

The beneficent force of enlightened individualism has been gaining
in strength during the past fifty years as evidenced by the life and
works of the great American leaders and statesmen such as Henry
George, William Jennings Bryan, George Norris and Robert M.
LaFollette Sr., to mention only a few. But it is since the depression
of the thirties and in consequence of the challenge contained in the
spread of Marxism in the world at large, that this force is manifesting itself in strong social tendencies which bear promise of a
solution of the problem of harmonizing the interests of the individual
with that of the social aggregate in a pragmatic American way. The
significant feature of these trends is that they continued in the post
war era despite what might have been the weakening factor of continued prosperity. Possibly the best indication of the strength of these
social tendencies is the frenzy which the disciples of rugged individualism work themselves into over the "social welfare" state, the
"hand-out" state, the "socialist" state, etc.

That these social tendencies are facilitating our efforts to deal
with the problem of the concentration of economic power is shown by
the fact that, despite the powerful hold of monopoly on our life, with
the unlimited possibility for pressure on legislation which this power
implies, and despite serious defects in the anti-monopoly laws the
enforcement of antitrust legislation has been showing increasing
vitality during the past sixteen years. Aside from the fact that, as is
generally acknowledged, the existence of the Sherman Antitrust Act
has prevented a complete cartelization of our economy on the British
model, the Antitrust Division of the United States Department of
Justice has, until the Korean war, expanded its work into the field
of concentration of economic power instead of limiting itself to the
prosecution of isolated instances of collusion. Moreover, despite the
handicaps imposed by an antiquated procedure of court litigation

and the complexity of the economico-juridical aspects of antitrust cases, court decisions have become increasingly favorable to the government.

The growth of a social atmosphere congenial to the work of the antitrust division is also evidenced by the extensive congressional investigations into the status of the monopoly problem which have been made in recent years, notably by the Temporary National Economic Committee of the United States Senate, the Small Business Committee of the House of Representatives and the latest investigating body, the "Subcommittee on the Study of Monopoly Power" of the Committee on the Judiciary of the House of Representatives (81st Congress). The truly remarkable increase which has taken place within recent years in the number of authoritative works which deal with monopoly and in the discussion of this subject in scholarly and popular periodicals should be also considered as indicative of the formation of a more favorable social atmosphere for anti-monopolistic activities. A significant evidence of the increasing social awareness of the monopoly problem is the first systematic effort to enforce a state antitrust law by the Antitrust Division of the State of Wisconsin which is engaged upon a vigorous enforcement of the state's antitrust act — an act which was passed in 1893 but which lay dormant until 1947 when the state's antitrust division was established through a special act of the Legislature.

Social Trends and the Law of Causality

The essential characteristic of the social trends which are at work in American society is that they afford the American people an increasing opportunity to influence their environment by directing the operation of the law of causality into channels consistent with the traditional American concept of the process of social improvement. As contrasted with the Soviet Union where the law of causality is made to function through government pressure, the American people are making progress, despite temporary setbacks, through social legislation in influencing the working of this law in a direction compatible with their ideals through the potency of their own democratic institutions.

In the Soviet Union it is considered, in accordance with the Marxian theory, that the economic rights of the individual are secured when they are merged in the economic rights of society through the socialization of the means of production and distribution. The Soviet Union has established a causal relation between the socialization of the basic economic resources and social welfare. This is their article of faith and no discussion of any other views concerning the relation between social welfare and other forms of ownership is possible. The American social philosophy, on the other hand, is grounded in the concept of the causal relation between social welfare and the private ownership of economic resources subject to the free play of competitive forces. The result is that in this country economic thinking presents a variegated picture as contrasted with the thinking which obtains in the Soviet Union with regard to the basic economic problems of access to economic resources.

While we, in this country, have irrevocably established as a foundation of our economy the principle of the causal relation between social welfare and individual economic freedom, we give free field, in accordance with our democratic concepts, to the expression of whatever views anyone can hold with respect to the causal interdependence between social welfare and any form of economic organization. As a consequence in our efforts to develop opportunities for the working of the competitive system we must wade through all sorts of formulations of causal sequences in social relationships and this frequently serves to befuddle the minds of the people and of the Congress as to the real issues at stake.

The Myth of Large-Scale Production

Possibly the most serious obstacle which the antitrust division encounters in its work is presented by the fatalistic nature of the theory entertained by many, if not most of our outstanding economists, of the inexorable drive towards large-scale production as it leads to centralization and integration of economic functions — a theory which forms the credo of the Marxian philosophy of economics. It is probable, however, that this view is one of those innumerable myths which have hindered in the past progressive development of mankind. In an address delivered before the 1947 convention of the American Economic Association, Senator (then Congressman) Estes Kefauver, in enumerating the grounds for his belief in antitrust policy, referred to Dr. Blair's views concerning "decentralizing techniques". . ."The thesis advanced by Dr. Blair," said Senator Kefauver, "that technology is now moving in the direction of smaller rather than large-scale operations certainly derives support from numerous instances which I personally have observed in my own region, the Tennessee Valley. Aided by low-cost electric power (which Dr. Blair lists as a major decentralizing technique), many relatively small enterprises have become established in the Valley and have been successful in their competition with much larger enterprises." [1]

In the words of Dr. Blair: "I personally subscribe very whole-heartedly to the view of the Committee of Economic Advisors as expressed in the Economic Report of the President as of January of this year [1950], in which it was pointed out that there is reason to believe that in many fields, size has thus far transcended the point required for optimum efficiency, and when size passes beyond that point there remains little economic justification for size." [2]

A recent report by the Federal Trade Commission enbodying the results of an investigation into the concentration of industry based on the 1947 Census of Manufacturers throws considerable light on the problem of size and methods to deal with it. The report upholds that for *certain* industries "a high degree of concentration is merely the inevitable consequence of the requirements of modern technology." But it also upholds that for *certain other* industries company concentration is not based upon large plants and could be substantially reduced without impairing whatever productive efficiency large plants achieve." [3]

In industry where both plant and company concentration are low — the more decentralized industries — the report says that "the task of protecting the public interest appears to be primarily that of preventing collusive agreements and arresting any such increase in company concentration as may tend to lessen competition." [4]

As to industries in which company concentration is high and is also appreciably greater than plant concentration, the report warns that "there is need to guard against not merely collusive agreement but also monopoly . . . If monopoly should be found to exist, the available remedies include the possibility of reducing the size of the largest business concerns." [5]

But there are still other industries where high company concentration is accompanied by high plant concentration, according to the report, so that "monopolistic concentration cannot readily be corrected by dissolution of monopolistic business firms but must be remedied instead by appropriate correction, or, if necessary, by regulation of business behavior." [6]

The development of efficient competitive enterprises can moreover become a reality if we consider that there is a large and rich region in the United States which is open to pioneer industrial development — the West — as is brought out by Wendell Berge in his study "Economic Freedom for the West." Mr. Berge's study opens new horizons to the American people in the re-creation of a new frontier which is to be conquered through industrial exploitation of our hitherto untouched — except for the few years of the war — Western Empire.

But as in every other phase of industrial activities the primary obstacle to such exploitation lies, as Mr. Berge shows, in monopolistic restrictions.

"Free enterprise, says Mr. Berge, is the key which can unlock the combination of resources, people, markets and new industries for the West. Monopoly, in all of its retarding effects, is the barrier which must be pierced before development can occur. In this conflict there can be no question that the west will have the active encouragement of people everywhere." [7]

Thus, whatever suggestions are made, they invariably revolve around the question of free competition as a prerequisite for the expansion of industrial activities — even to new territories. Such expansion presents a problem of momentous importance in view of the coming on the market of a new labor force every year. This new labor force must find employment in a way consistent with the dignity of American citizens, not through handouts in the form of artificially devised public works of the CWA, WPA and other injections into our economic body, but through a systematic capacity exploitation of our present industrial facilities and of those that lie dormant in some of our richest regions.

In concluding his book *Economic Freedom for the West* Wendell Berge says: "It is to be hoped that the evidence presented throughout these pages makes clear that the continuing crux of both the industrial policies of government and the behavior of industry itself pivots upon the presence or absence of monopoly. The triumph of monopoly would in time become the nemesis of our system of free enterprise. Domination of the market, regimentation by private economic governments, and all of the attendant varieties of discrimination which characterize monopoly are not only paradoxes to be examined academically; they are a menace, whose perpetuation we cannot brook." [8]

Antitrust legislation and adequate enforcement appear as the media which can counteract the pressure of fatalistic economic forces in the only possible way consistent with the American tradition and the American outlook on life. The social atmosphere which is being formed in the nation holds out hope for the possibility of solving the problem of the concentration of economic power not through revolutionary action but through the administration of laws which express the American pragmatic philosophy of evolutionary changes from the lower to the higher forms of social relationships.

"The lessons of history," says Professor Vernon A. Mund, "clearly indicate that competition is effectively realized only when government takes steps to create and maintain it. When the efforts of government to preserve and restore competition are weak, the profit-seeking interest of enterprisers gives rise to an amazing variety of restrictions, restraints, and collusive actions designed to avoid competition and exclude competitors." [9]

The interest which was aroused in recent years in the Sherman Antitrust Act as an instrument by which the government seeks to preserve and restore competition, brought out a number of weaknesses in it. The act needs undoubtedly considerable strengthening and even, as Dr. Levi points out, it may need a new interpretation and "an increased awareness of the responsibility of the courts to give adequate relief." [10] But whatever the situation, the fact is that antitrust legislation offers the only possibility of bringing about a competitive accessibility to economic resources — an essential condition of a normal functioning of a competitive economic organization.

Considering that legislation in a democracy is the only medium for a conscious control of the social environment, the strengthening of antitrust legislation is imperative to enable us to counteract the action of those inexorable forces which in the Marxian view ride over national ideals and aspirations. Our distinctive attitude towards life as it was formed by our tradition rests on our awareness of the presence of a subjective force which, if given opportunities to assert itself, should in the long run overpower the fatalistic drive of objective environmental forces.

The vitality of social trends is difficult to appraise. Social trends are the expression of warring social forces; they are the manifestations of a conflict between the old, which has outlived its usefulness, and the new, which is struggling to harmonize economic relationships with changed objective conditions. Rugged individualism which played a determining role in the physical development of this continent is at grips with the forces of enlightened individualism which are working towards the preservation of the traditional American concept of economic freedom against the encroachment of concentrated economic power — the economic consequences of rugged individualism. This struggle is marked by occasional setbacks for social legislation which embodies the concept of enlightened individualism. The strength and vitality of this legislation can be presumed to be insured by the interplay of three factors: our traditional spirit of freedom; the lasting impression of the depression of the Thirties on the American people, and the threat of social and economic theories which are inimical to our concept of economics and our way-of-life and which are being grafted on a large part of the population of the globe.

With the inauguration of a war economy the American people are faced with the problem of withstanding the action of the fatalistic forces which in times of national danger are given free rein and which, as the experience of World War II shows, will lead us to a greater concentration of economic power. It is of prime importance that we organize our national defense in the economic field in such a manner as to preserve our traditional economic ideals and our time-honored way-of-life.

[*] Apart from a relatively short period under the administrations of Presidents Theodore Roosevelt and William Howard Taft.
[1] Estes Kefauver, "Needed Changes in Legislation," *American Economic Review*, May, 1948, p. 184.
[2] *Hearings before the Subcommittee of Monopoly Power of the Committee on the Judiciary*, House of Representatives, 81st Congress, p. 201, Serial No. 14, Part I.
[3] Federal Trade Commission Report, 1947 Census of Manufacturers, p. 14.
[4] *Ibid.*, p. 35.
[5] *Ibid.*, p. 35.
[6] *Ibid.*, p. 35.
[7] Wendell Berge, *Economic Freedom for the West*, p. 6.
[8] Wendell Berge, *Economic Freedom for the West*, p. 141.
[9] Vernon A. Mund, *Government and Business*, Harper, New York, 1950, p. 112.
[10] Edward H. Levi, "The Antitrust Laws and Monopoly," *The Chicago Law Review*, February, 1947, p. 183.